BOOKS BY JOSEPH WOOD KRUTCH

a selected list

The Modern Temper
Samuel Johnson
Henry David Thoreau
The Twelve Seasons
The Desert Year
The Best of Two Worlds
More Lives Than One

Editor of Great American Nature Writing

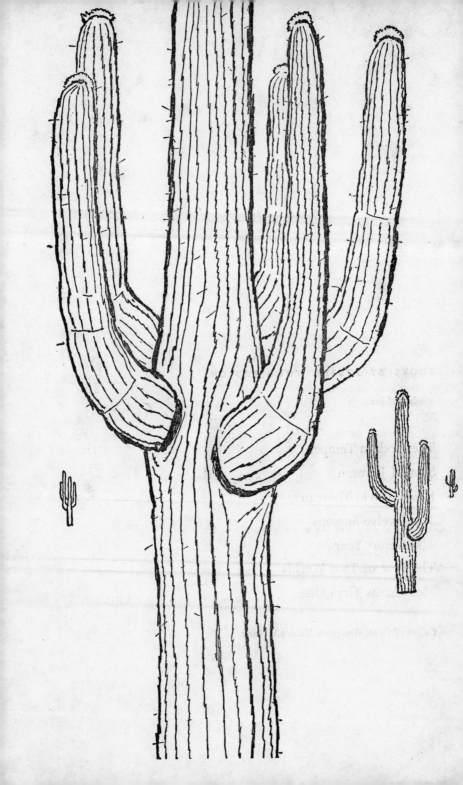

JOSEPH WOOD KRUTCH

he voice of the

desert

NATURALIST'S INTERPRETATION

WILLIAM SLOANE ASSOCIATES

NEW YORK

Fourth Printing, January 1971

Gratetul acknowledgment is made to the following periodicals for permission to reprint material which appeared originally in their pages:

The American Scholar, for "Conservation Is Not Enough" and "He Was There Before Coronado"
The Virginia Quarterly Review, for "The Moth and the Candle"

DESIGNED BY MARSHALL LEE

to the memory of Margaret Pickel and Numa Zinty

The author thanks Professor Lyman Benson of Pomona College for reading the chapter on the development of the cacti. He is not, however, responsible for any of the statements made.

ONE

the what and the why
of desert country

ON THE BRIGHTEST AND WARMEST DAYS MY DESERT IS MOST
itself because sunshine and warmth are the very essence
of its character. The air is lambent with light; the caress-
ing warmth envelops everything in its ardent embrace.
Even when outlanders complain that the sun is too daz-
zling and too hot, we desert lovers are prone to reply,
"At worst that is only too much of a good thing."

Unfortunately, this is the time when the tourist is least
likely to see it. Even the winter visitor who comes for a
month or six weeks is mostly likely to choose January or

February because he is thinking about what he is escaping at home rather than of what he is coming to here. True, the still warm sun and the usually bright skies make a dramatic contrast with what he has left behind. In the gardens of his hotel or guest ranch, flowers still bloom and some of the more obstreperous birds make cheerful sounds, even though they do not exactly sing at this season. The more enthusiastic visitors talk about "perpetual summer" and sometimes ask if we do not find the lack of seasons monotonous. But this is nonsense. Winter is winter even in the desert.

At Tucson's twenty-three hundred feet it often gets quite cold at night even though shade temperatures during the day may rise to seventy-five or even higher. Most vegetation is pausing, though few animals hibernate. This is a sort of neutral time when the desert environment is least characteristically itself. It is almost like late September or early October, just after the first frost, in southern New England. For those who are thinking of nothing except getting away from something, rather than learning to know a new world, this is all very well. But you can't become acquainted with the desert itself at that time of year.

By April the desert is just beginning to come into its own. The air and the skies are summery without being hot; the roadsides and many of the desert flats are thickly carpeted with a profusion of wildflowers such as only California can rival. The desert is smiling before it begins to laugh, and October or November are much the same. But June is the month for those who want to know what the desert is really like. That is the time to decide once and for all if it is, as for many it turns out to be, "your country."

It so happens that I am writing this not long after the twenty-first of June and I took especial note of that astronomically significant date. This year summer began at precisely ten hours and no minutes, Mountain Standard Time. That means that the sun rose higher and stayed longer in the sky than on any other day of the year. In the north there is often a considerable lag in the seasons as the earth warms up, but here, where it is never very cold, the longest day and the hottest are likely to coincide pretty closely. So it was this year. On June 21 the sun rose almost to the zenith so that at noon he cast almost no shadow. And he was showing what he is capable of.

Even in this dry air 109° Fahrenheit in the shade is pretty warm. Under the open sky the sun's rays strike with an almost physical force, pouring down from a blue dome unmarked by the faintest suspicion of even a fleck of cloud. The year has been unusually dry even for the desert. During the four months just past no rain—not even a light shower—has fallen. The surface of the ground is as dry as powder. And yet, when I look out of the window the dominant color of the landscape is incredibly green.

On the low foothills surrounding the steep rocky slopes of the mountains, which are actually ten or twelve miles away but seem in the clear air much closer at hand, this greenness ends in a curving line following the contour of the mountains' base and inevitably suggesting the waves of a green sea lapping the irregular shore line of some island rising abruptly from the ocean. Between me and that shore line the desert is sprinkled with hundreds, probably thousands, of evenly placed shrubs, varied now and then by a small tree—usually a mesquite or what is called locally a cat's-claw acacia.

More than a month ago all the little annual flowers and weeds which spring up after the winter rains and rush from seed to seed again in six weeks gave up the ghost at the end of their short lives. Their hope of posterity lies now invisible, either upon the surface of the bare ground or just below it. Yet when the summer thunderstorms come in late July or August, they will not make the mistake of germinating. They are triggered to explode into life only when they are both moist and cool—which they will not be until next February or March when their season begins. Neither the shrubs nor the trees seem to know that no rain has fallen during the long months. The leathery, somewhat resinous, leaves of the dominant shrub—the attractive plant unattractively dubbed "creosote bush"—are not at all parched or wilted. Neither are the deciduous leaves of the mesquite.

Not many months ago the creosote was covered with bright yellow pealike flowers; the mesquite with pale yellow catkins. Now the former is heavy with gray seed and on the mesquite are forming long pods which Indians once ate and which cattle now find an unusually rich food.

It looks almost as though the shrubs and trees could live without water. But of course they cannot. Every desert plant has its secret, though it is not always the same one. In the case of the mesquite and the creosote it is that their roots go deep and that, so the ecologists say, there is in the desert no wet or dry season below six feet. What little moisture is there is pretty constant through the seasons of the year and through the dry years as well as the wet. Like the temperature in some caves, it never varies. The mesquite and creosote are not compelled to care whether it has rained for four months or not. And unlike many other plants they flourish whether there has been less rain or more than usual.

Those plants which have substantial root systems but nevertheless do not reach so deep are more exuberant some years than others. Thus the Encelia, or brittlebush, which, in normal years, literally covers many slopes with thousands of yellow, daisy-like flowers, demands a normal year. Though I have never seen it fail, I am told that in very dry years it comes into leaf but does not flower, while in really catastrophic droughts it does not come up at all, as the roots lie dormant and hope for better times. Even the creosote bush, which never fails, can, nevertheless, profit from surface water, and when it gets the benefit of a few thunderstorms in late July or August, it will flower and fruit a second time so that the expanse which is now all green will be again sprinkled with yellow.

On such a day as this even the lizards, so I have noticed, hug the thin shade of the bushes. If I venture out, the zebratails scurry indignantly away, the boldly banded appendages which give them their name curved high over their backs. But I don't venture out very often during the middle of the day. It is more pleasant to sit inside where a cooler keeps the house at a pleasant eighty degrees. And if you think that an advocate of the simple life should not succumb to a cooler, it is you rather than I who is inconsistent. Even Thoreau had a fire in his cottage at Walden and it is no more effete to cool oneself in a hot climate than it is to get warm before a stove in a cold one. The gadget involved is newer, but that is all.

In this country "inclemency" means heat. One is "sunbound" instead of snowbound and I have often noticed

that the psychological effect is curiously similar. It is cozy
to be shut in, to have a good excuse for looking out of the
window or into oneself. A really blazing day slows down
the restless activity of a community very much as a blizzard does in regions which have them. Without the one or
the other any society, I imagine, would become intoler-
ably extroverted. Where there is either, a sort of meteor-
ological sabbath is usually observed even by those who
keep no other.

In Connecticut the chickadees came to see me when I
did not go to see them. In Arizona the desert birds do the
same, though the attraction—which was certainly not me
in either case—is water rather than food. A curved-billed
thrasher, his threatening beak half-open like the mouth of
a panting dog, approaches defiantly, scattering the smaller
birds as he comes. A cactus wren, the largest and boldest
of the wren tribe, impudently invades my porch and even
jumps to a window sill to peer at me through the glass.
And as I know from experience, he will invade even the
house if I leave a door open and will carry away for his
nest any material available. Only the large white-winged
dove does not seem to notice that this is an unusually
warm day. He will fly away to Mexico at the first hint that
summer is over and now, when the temperature in the sun
must be at least 120 degrees, he seems to be saying, "But
we don't call this hot in Campeche."

From my window I see also the furry and the scaly as
well as the feathered. A jack rabbit approaches cautiously
and after looking carefully about dares to lower his head
long enough to take a long drink; a few minutes later a
lizard does the same. What did either do before I kept a
vessel always full? Most of the time, I imagine, they did

without. But like human beings who have access to conveniences and luxuries, they probably prefer to do with.

Obviously the animals and plants who share this country with me take it for granted. To them it is just "the way things are." By now I am beginning to take it for granted myself. But being a man I must ask what they cannot: What *is* a desert and why is it what it is? At latitude thirty-two one expects the climate to be warm. But the desert is much more than merely warm. It is a consistent world with a special landscape, a special geography, and, to go with them, a special flora and fauna adapted to that geography and that climate.

Nearly every striking feature of this special world, whether it be the shape of the mountains or the habits of its plant and animal inhabitants, goes back ultimately to the grand fact of dryness—the dryness of the ground, of the air, of the whole sum-total. And the most inclusive cause of the dryness is simply that out here it doesn't rain very much.

Some comparisons with regions where it rains more may help us understand what that means. Take, for example, southern New England. By world standards it gets a lot—namely some forty inches of rain per year. Certain parts of the southern states get even more: about fifty inches for east Tennessee, nearly sixty for New Orleans. Some areas on the West Coast get fantastic amounts, like the seventy-five inches at Crescent City, California, and the unbelievable 153 inches, or nearly four times what New York City gets, recorded one year in Del Norde County, California.

Nevertheless, New England's forty is a lot of water,

either comparatively or absolutely. The region around
Paris, for instance, gets little more than half that amount.
Forty inches is, in absolute terms, more than most people
imagine. One inch of rain falling on an acre of ground
means more than 27,000 gallons of water. No wonder that
irrigation in dry regions is quite a formidable task even for
modern technology.

In terms of what vegetation can use, forty inches is
ample for the kind of agriculture and natural growth
which we tend to think of as "normal." It means luxuriant
grass, rapid development of second growth woodland,
a veritable jungle of weeds and bushes in midsummer. In
inland America the rainfall tends to be less than in the
coastal regions. As one moves westward from the Mississippi it declines sharply and begins to drop below twenty
inches a year at about the one hundredth meridian or,
very roughly, at a line drawn from Columbus, Ohio
through Oklahoma City. This means too little water for
most broad-leaved trees and explains why the southern
Great Plains were as treeless when the white man first saw
them as they are today.

Our true deserts—the Great Basin Desert in Utah and
Nevada, the Chihuahuan in New Mexico, the Sonoran in
Arizona, and the Mohave in California—all lie still further
to the west. The four differ among themselves but they
are all dry and hot and they all fulfill what is probably
the most satisfactory definition of "desert"—namely a region where the ground cover is not continuous; where,
that is, the earth remains bare of vegetation between such
plants as manage to grow. Over these American deserts
the rainfall varies considerably and with it the character
and extent of the vegetation. In southern Arizona, for in-

stance, it is about four inches at Yuma, nearly eleven near
Tucson. Four inches means sand dunes which look like
those pictures of the Sahara which the word "desert" calls
to most people's minds. Eleven means that where the soil
is suitable, well-separated individuals of such desert plants
as the cacti and the paloverde trees will flourish.

But if scanty rainfall makes for deserts, what makes for
scanty rainfall? To that there are two important answers.
One is simply that most regions other than the mountain-
ous ones tend to be dry if they lie in that belt of permanently high atmospheric pressure which extends some
thirty or thirty-five degrees on each side of the equator
where calms are frequent and winds erratic. Old sailors
used to call this region "the horse latitudes" though nobody knows why and you can take your choice of three
equally unconvincing explanations. One is that it was because horses tended to die when the ships lay long in the
hot calms. Another, because the boisterous changeable-
ness of the winds when they do come suggests unruly
horses. A third is that they were originally called after the
English explorer, Ross, which was mistaken by the Ger-
mans for their old word for "horse." In any event, the
latitude of Tucson puts it just within the "horse latitudes."
Most of the important deserts of the world, including the
Sahara and the Gobi, lie within this same belt.

The other important answer to the question, "What
makes for scanty rainfall?" is, "Mountains lying across the
path of such moist winds as do blow." In our case the
Coast Ranges of California lie between us and the Pacific.
From my front porch, which looks directly across the
desert to some nearer mountains of the southernmost
Rockies, I can see, on a small scale, what happens. Many,

many times a moisture-laden mass of air reaches as far as these closest mountains. Dark clouds form, sometimes the whole range is blotted out. Torrential rains are falling. But on me not a drop. Either the sky is blue overhead or the high clouds which have blown my way dissolve visibly as the warm air rising from my sun-drenched flats reaches them. I am in what the geographers call a "rain shadow" cast by the mountains. Up at their summit the rainfall is nearly twice as much as it is down here and they are clothed with pines beginning at six or seven thousand feet and going on up to the nine-thousand-foot peak. When I do get rain in midwinter and in midsummer, it is usually because winds have brought moisture up from the Gulf of Mexico by an unobstructed southern route, or because in summer a purely local thundershower has been formed out of the hot air rising from the sun-beaten desert floor. Most of the time the sun is hot, even in winter, and the air is usually fantastically dry, the relative humidity being often less than ten.

Naturally the plants and animals living in such a region must be specially adapted to survive under such conditions, but the casual visitor usually notices the strangeness of the landscape before he is aware of the flora or the fauna. And the peculiar features of the landscape are also the result of dryness, even in ways that are not immediately obvious.

The nude mountains reveal their contours, or veil them as lightly as the late Greek sculptors veiled their nudes, because only near the summits of the mountains can anything tall enough to obscure the outlines grow. A little less obvious is the fact that the beautiful "monuments" of northern Arizona and southern Utah owe their unusual forms to the sculpturing of wind-blown sand, or that sheer cliffs often rise from a sloping cone of rocks and boulders because the talus slopes can accumulate in just that way only where there is not enough draining water to distribute them over the whole surrounding plain, as they would be distributed in regions of heavier rainfall. But the most striking example of all is the greatest single scenic wonder of the region, the Grand Canyon itself. This narrow gash, cut a mile deep through successive strata until the river flows at last over some of the oldest rock exposed anywhere on earth, could have been formed only in a very dry climate.

As recently as two hundred years ago the best informed observer would have taken it for granted that the river was running between those sheer walls at the bottom of the gorge simply because it had found them out. Today few visitors are not aware that the truth lies the other way around, that the river cut its own course through the rock. But most laymen do not ask the next questions: Why is Grand Canyon unique, or why are such canyons, even on a smaller scale, rare? And the answer to those questions is that a set of very special conditions was necessary.

First there must be a thick series of rock strata slowly rising as a considerable river flows over it. Second, that considerable river must carry an unusual amount of hard sand or stone fragments in suspension so that it will be able to cut downward at least as rapidly as the rock over which it flows is rising. Third, that considerable river must be flowing through very arid country. Otherwise rain, washing over the edges of the cut, will widen it at the top as the cut goes deeper. That is why broad valleys are characteristic of regions with normal rainfall; canyons, large and small, of arid country.

And Grand Canyon is the grandest of all canyons because at that particular place all the necessary conditions were fulfilled more exuberantly than at any other place in the whole world. The Colorado River carries water from a relatively wet country through a dry one, it bears with it a fantastic amount of abrasive material, the rock over which it flows has been slowly rising during several millions of years, and too little rain falls to widen very rapidly the gash which it cuts. Thus in desert country everything from the color of a mouse or the shape of a leaf up to the largest features of the mountains themselves is more likely than not to have the same explanation: dryness.

So far as living things go, all this adds up to what even an ecologist may so far forget himself as to call an "unfavorable environment." But like all such pronouncements this one doesn't mean much unless we ask "unfavorable for what and for whom?" For many plants, for many animals, and for some men it is very favorable indeed. Many of the first two would languish and die, transferred to some region where conditions were "more favorable." It is here, and here only, that they flourish. Many men feel healthier and happier in the bright dry air than they do anywhere else. And since I happen to be one of them, I not unnaturally have a special interest in the plants and animals who share my liking for just these conditions. For five years now I have been amusing myself by inquiring of them directly what habits and what adjustments they have found most satisfactory. Many of them are delightfully ingenious and eminently sensible.

The "hard" conditions they sometimes have to cope with appear to strangers much more difficult than they are, merely because they are not those to which the strangers are accustomed. After all, few environments are entirely favorable. No one out in a blizzard or ice storm in southern New England is likely to think of it as calculated to coddle man, beast or vegetable. For months in a New England winter, every living thing has been on the desperate defensive; most have temporarily given up the struggle and are lying low. A great many will never revive from the inanition into which they have sunk. In the desert, heat and drought are no more difficult to survive. Some of the techniques of survival are different, some are surprisingly similar to those which are used to cope with cold.

We human beings are not very rugged as living organisms go. In fact we are extraordinarily tender creatures who can exist even uncomfortably only within a very narrow range of temperature and only if protected from most of the manifestations of nature. In the New England winter we warm ourselves with fires and if we go out we bundle ourselves up in wool or even in rubber to ward off cold and dampness. We think it nothing extraordinary to stay all day in the house because the weather is a little more unfavorable than usual. In the desert the only difference is that the inclemencies from which we protect ourselves are different. If we tend to keep out of the sun in midsummer, occasionally even stay in the house almost all day because it is too hot to go out, inhabitants of the so-called temperate regions are compelled even more frequently to keep out of the cold and the wet. Actually we are considerably less at the mercy of the elements than they are.

Men of most races have long been accustomed to speak
with scorn of the few peoples who happen to live where
nature makes things too easy. In the inclemency of their
weather, the stoniness of their soil, or the rigors of their
winter they find secret virtues so that even the London
fog has occasionally found Englishmen to praise it. No
doubt part of all this is mere prejudice at worst, making
a virtue out of necessity at best. But undoubtedly there
is also something in it. We grow strong against the pressure of a difficulty, and ingenious by solving problems.
Individuality and character are developed by challenge.
We tend to admire trees, as well as men, who bear the
stamp of their successful struggles with a certain amount
of adversity. People who have not had too easy a time of
it develop flavor. And there is no doubt about the fact
that desert life has character. Plants and animals are so
obviously and visibly what they are because of the problems they have solved. They are part of some whole. They
belong. Animals and plants, as well as men, become especially interesting when they do fit their environment,
when to some extent they reveal what their response to
it has been. And nowhere more than in the desert do they
reveal it.

I have lived in this house and been lord of these few
acres for nearly five years and the creatures who share the
desert with me have already summed me up as a softy
and have grown contemptuously familiar. It is not only
that the cactus wrens sit on the backs of my porch chairs.
The round-tailed ground squirrels—plain, sand-colored,
chipmunk-like animals—are digging rather too many burrows rather too close about the house. The jack rabbits
—normally the most timid as well as the fleetest of crea-

tures—take nibbles at the few plants I have set out and refuse to leave off until I arrive shouting and waving my arms a few feet from where they are. Sooner or later something may have to be done to discourage this impudent familiarity, but for the present I am getting some good looks at creatures who usually don't wait to be looked at. Yesterday, for instance, I saw what at first I thought was a bird eating seeds from the upper branches of a creosote bush. It turned out to be a ground squirrel belying his name by climbing several feet above ground among the slender swaying branches of the creosote to eat the small fuzzy seeds. This is doubtless no addition to Knowledge with a capital K. But it is an addition to my knowledge and that is the next best thing. I like to investigate such matters for myself when I can. "What on earth do they live on?" is a common question from those newcomers not too egotistical to notice that creatures other than those of their own kind do live here somehow. Obviously "creosote seeds" is one answer so far as the ground squirrel is concerned.

T W O

it suits him fine

NOT ALL THE ANSWERS I GET WHEN I ASK THE QUESTION
"How do you live in the desert?" are as simple as that of
the ground squirrel who does not stay on the ground.
What then are some of the others?

Some creatures, it must be admitted, behave like the
pampered part-time human inhabitants who run away to
the mountains when the desert is being most exuberantly
itself. These I tolerate as I do their human analogues. But
it is we year-round residents who interest me most. And
I soon noticed one grand persistent difference between the

plants and animals who do stick it out and those of us human beings who seem to do the same.

As usual, the animals are healthy and happy because they have adapted themselves to the environment. As usual, man is healthy and happy because even when, like me, he prides himself on being not too timid about those aspects of nature which are not familiar, he has modified the environment to make it conform to his own fixed needs. Man can change things as no other animal can. But by way of compensation he can change himself much less.

Of that difference and what it implies we shall perhaps have something to say later on, but it is obvious that his method implies penalties as well as advantages and in the long run the penalties may count for more than he now suspects. For the moment, however, I am most interested in those creatures who have taken things as they found them and then found out how to find them good. It is surprising how many different ways there are of doing just that.

On the desk beside me as I write is a largish glass jar, its bottom covered with two inches of damp, sandy soil. In one corner, buried to the eyes and nose, is a small toad who has grown from half an inch to two inches long under my eyes. Occasionally he sits fully exposed on a miniature hillock and surveys his world. Most of the time, however, he prefers to remain covered or almost covered by the nice, soft mud.

While he was very small and I waved in front of him a microscopic piece of raw beef on the end of a broom-straw, he would seize it with absurd ferocity and, if it was rather large for the size of his gullet, he would use a front paw to stuff it down after the usual fashion of toads as I have observed them in places very different from this. For him and for many captive creatures, as well as for so many Americans, hamburger became the very staff of life. But like most of the reptiles and amphibia, he does not seem to take much pleasure in eating. It is a rather difficult business to be got over with as soon as possible, and his attitude has not changed much now that he has graduated from hamburger to living insects.

Small as he is, there is no difficulty in determining to what species he belongs. Exposed to bright light, the pupils of his eyes contract to vertical ellipses like the eyes of a cat, and that fact suggests that he is one of the spadefoot toads. The tiny speck of black horny tissue on each hind foot clinches the matter. Moreover, since these "spades" are crescent rather than wedge shaped, he stands revealed as the Sonoran spadefoot or, more formally, Scaphiopus couchii. When he is grown his spades will be only a few millimeters long, but they will help him to become a phenomenal digger.

He has been my guest for some ten months now and it was one of his kind who gave me one of my big surprises during my first summer in the desert. One evening after a heavy thundershower, the air was suddenly filled with mysterious nasal "baas" and a flashlight revealed hundreds of the small toads disporting themselves amorously and otherwise in the unusual wetness. Two nights later they had disappeared completely and were not to be seen again until the next year.

Even during most of the short, relatively wet season, adults are not seen except rarely, though for one or two nights the surface of the earth literally swarms with those who have come forth from somewhere to celebrate their pervigilium veneris. The young are not quite so scarce during a few months after they are hatched, but I count myself very lucky to have found my specimen by accident near a well-watered trench around some shrubs a few feet away from my door. For one thing this proves—and even this has not been recorded in the almost nonexistent scientific literature about the Sonoran spadefoot—that at least the very young toadlets do not always dig in immediately. For another thing, I have been able to observe his behavior during the months when his fellows seem to have disappeared from the earth. And that, it appears, has seldom been done.

I feel certain that I know almost to a day how old he is. One late afternoon last July we had our first real thundershower and I said to myself, "Tonight the spadefoots will sing." And of course they did. Next day I searched the area where I had seen them, hoping to find at least one rain puddle which had lasted long enough to hatch the eggs. I knew from previous experience that they are often laid in such puddles and require only about twenty-four hours to hatch. Less lucky than I had been on my first summer, I found none. But some there must have been, because here is the young toad apparently very comfortable indeed in the jar on my desk. After that July night there were at least three heavier showers, but the spadefoots, having had their night, put in no second appearance.

Except for his age I do not know much about my specimen. Neither, apparently, does anyone else know either how he has spent his time between the days when the tadpole transformed itself with remarkable celerity into a toad and the time when I took charge, or how, had he been left to his own devices, he would have spent the months until the next July. The ancient belief that many lowly creatures were simply born every year out of the mud would seem, on the face of things, to get its strongest support right here.

Those writers of textbooks and manuals who are compelled to say something about Scaphiopus couchii seem agreed that he must spend the major part of his time buried somewhere in the earth. But where, under what conditions, and doing what (if anything) nobody knows. Already, however, I think I am beginning to have evidence which permits certain presumptions. Perhaps if I get more I shall some day return to the subject. But I introduce him now for a different reason, which is this: Without knowing any more than I already do, it is clear enough that the spadefoot represents, in a very extreme form, one of the ways of living in the desert—namely by lying low most of the time.

Many plants do the same. They exist only as seeds during all but about six weeks out of the fifty-two. And though it seems less extraordinary for a plant to do this than it does for an animal to remain buried for an even greater proportion of the time, the analogy is obvious and will remain so, even if it should turn out that the spadefoot's inactivity is not so nearly absolute as has sometimes been assumed.

Now one might object that in the case of this toad what we have is not really an example of how to live in the desert, but merely of how to survive there by surrendering ninety-nine hundredths of one's supposed right to live. It might seem to give the lie to my rash contention that for desert creatures the desert is not "an unfavorable environment."

Instead of disputing this point, it would be better to admit right away that quite a few other creatures either elude the problems which desert living presents, or are so cosmopolitanly undemanding that they get along very well either in the desert or in a quite different environment. Within the desert states there are, for instance, several toads other than the spadefoot, though most of them, instead of managing as he does to survive in the desert itself, confine themselves to areas which happen for one reason or another to be undesert-like. The Colorado River toad— commonly seven inches long and quite the largest of his kind in the United States—is a notable example who sticks pretty close to water holes, natural or artificial; one finds him about swimming pools in desert homes or water holes maintained for cattle on the ranches, and to this habit he owes his local name cow toad. As the most recent textbook, Stebbins' *Amphibians of Western North America,* says of him: "Dwells in arid regions but appears to be dependent, to a considerable extent, upon the presence of permanent springs or streams. Has entered the Imperial Valley of California with the development of irrigation." In other words the cow toad spreads when man makes the desert less desert-like. The road runner does not, as we shall see.

Or take the case of the familiar robin. You are not likely to find him in the desert, though he is common enough in the mountains at, say, five or six thousand feet where the vegetation and climate are approximately that of the more northerly parts of the United States. Yet I once saw a robin on a tiny patch of grass not more than ten by twenty feet in size but carefully nursed by the owner of a rather large house. The robin was digging for worms for all the world as though he were on a New England lawn and any worms he found had been introduced by man. No doubt if large estates with artificially sustained lawns and trees were more numerous and closer together than they are, then the robins would move in.

Still other creatures range naturally over vast and vastly different areas simply because the few things indispensable to them are found everywhere, even in desert areas. Not too long ago, for instance, a neighbor brought me a large bat which had fallen into his swimming pool. Neighbors are very generous with such gifts once they know that you are willing to take the responsibility for them, and this one I was glad to get. He rested for a while hanging upside down in a cardboard box and then flew away, apparently none the worse for his experience. But what interested me particularly was the fact that, though I had never before seen out here this particular sort of bat close enough to recognize him, the white-tipped fur of his back was enough to identify him as the hoary bat which is found all over the United States except for the southern tip of Florida, and which ranges well northward into Canada. Like our other native bats, he is dependent upon flying insects for food and that means that he must either hibernate in winter or fly south to some place where insects are on the wing the year around. But grant the hoary bat his necessary food, and it appears that mountains, valleys, plains and even deserts are all one to him.

Ecologists like to "explain" the survival of a particular animal or plant by noting its various "fitnesses." One creature, so they say, is peculiarly adapted to the temperature or the food supply of a certain region. This other one produces a great number of offspring; this third species gives exceptionally effective care to its one or two young, etc., etc. All these statements are usually true enough, but there are so many ways of surviving that there are almost as many different explanations as there are different creatures. But since we are interested in the problem of how to live in the desert, the most interesting answers are not those which are really how to live almost anywhere, and that is, after all, the answer the hoary bat is prepared to give.

To find an answer to the more interesting question; to find an animal which refuses to live anywhere *except* in the desert; to find one which is, in his own peculiar way, very demanding even though what he demands is what most animals would not have at any price, I do not have to go far. Indeed, I do not have to go any further from my doorstep than I went to find the spadefoot. And it happens that I intruded upon this perfect desert dweller at a dramatic moment only a few days ago when I stepped out in the early morning and was startled by a large chicken-sized bird—if you can still call him a bird—who was dashing madly back and forth at right angles to my line of vision. His headlong plunges were so like those of a frenzied hen who seems to be rushing madly in all directions at once, that for a moment I thought I had frightened him out of his wits. As it turned out, he was merely too busy at the moment to acknowledge my presence.

As to *what* he was, that question could be answered by even the most unobservant person who has ever driven a highway in the desert. He was one of the commonest, as well as perhaps the most remarkable, of all desert birds

—namely a road runner—nearly two feet of relentless energy from the tip of his wicked bill to the tip of the long, expressive tail which may trail the ground when he is calm or depressed, or be raised almost as straight up as the tail of a confident cat when he is happily angry, as indeed he seems to be a good part of the time. From his bold bad eye to his springy tread everything proclaims him "rascal," and he has, in truth, a number of bad habits. But there is also something indescribably comic about him, and he illustrates the rule that comic rascals have a way of engaging the affection of even the virtuous. Nearly everybody is curiously cheered by the sight of a road runner. In the old days the cowboys used to be amused by his habit of racing ahead of their horses and they gave him his name. The Mexicans of Sonora call him affectionately "paisano" or "countryman."

My specimen, far from having lost his wits, had them very much about him. Suddenly he arrested his mad career, stabbed with lightning rapidity at the ground and, crest erect, lifted his head triumphantly—with a good sized lizard in his beak. No one who has ever seen one of our lizards run would like to be assigned the task of chasing it from bush to bush and then nabbing it with a hand. But catching lizards is all in a day's work for a road runner and mine was merely collecting some for his breakfast. His diet is varied from time to time by a snake, or even an insect, if the insect happens to be large enough to be worth the effort of a leap from the ground to take him on the wing, as I have seen a zooming dragonfly taken. Responsible observers say that when the lizard tries his usual trick of surrendering his tail so that the rest of him may make a safe getaway, the road runner, unlike some other predators, is not to be fooled. He merely takes a firmer grip on the body and collects the discarded tail later. Scorpions are also quite acceptable as tidbits.

Inevitably such a creature is the center of many legends. There seems to be no doubt that he takes the killing of rattlesnakes in his stride, but old-timers insist that he sometimes first surrounds the snake with a circle of spiny cactus joints so that the snake cannot get away. In fact, only a few weeks ago a friend told me that one of *his* friends had seen a slight variation on this performance when a road runner walled the snake in with small stones before attacking him. But like the milk snake milking a cow and the hoop snake rolling merrily along with his tail in his mouth, this remarkable performance seems never to be witnessed by anyone with a professional interest in natural history and it is usually a friend of a friend who was on the spot. The situation seems much the same as that with ghosts. You are most likely to see them if you are a simple person and have faith.

As a matter of fact, however, you do not always have to be a simple or ignorant person to believe what the simple tell you. A well-educated man recently passed on to me the old superstition that the Gila monster, our only poisonous lizard, owed his venom to the unfortunate fact that nature had not provided him with any orifice through which the waste products of metabolism could be discharged, and that poisons therefore inevitably accumulated. One need only turn a Gila on his back to dispose of this legend which is sufficiently improbable on the face of it. Most of the people who repeat it have pointlessly taken part in the attempt to exterminate these creatures, but have obviously never looked at the bodies of their victims. And yet we still feel superior to the men of the Middle Ages who insisted that the toad had a precious jewel in his head, when they might so easily have found out that he didn't!

Of course it may just possibly turn out that the road runner really does fence his victims in. Stranger things do happen and the evidence against it is necessarily only negative. But the "paisano" is odd enough without the legends. Almost everything about him is unbird-like at the same time that it fits him to desert conditions. He is a bird who has learned how not to act like one.

Though he can fly—at least well enough to get to the top of a mesquite if there is some really urgent reason for doing so—he would rather not, trusting to his long legs to catch his prey and to get him out of trouble. The sound which he makes is like nothing on earth, least of all like a bird. One writer describes it as a sort of modified Bronx cheer, which is right enough since it seems to be made by the raucous expelling of air accompanied by a rapid gnashing of the bill—if a bill can be gnashed. Like the bird himself, the sound is derisive, irascible, ribald, threatening, and highly self-confident. As befits a no-nonsense sort of creature, the road runner is content to dress himself in neutral, brown-speckled feathers, but there is a line of red cuticle behind his eye which he can expose when it seems desirable to look a bit fiercer than usual.

Sociologists talk a great deal these days about "adjustment," which has always seemed to me a defeatist sort of word suggesting dismal surrender to the just tolerable. The road runner is not "adjusted" to his environment. He is triumphant in it. The desert is his home and he likes it. Other creatures, including many other birds, elude and

compromise. They cling to the mountains or to the cot-
tonwood-filled washes, especially in the hot weather, or
they go away somewhere else, like the not entirely reconciled human inhabitants of this region. The road runner,
on the other hand, stays here all the time and he prefers
the areas where he is hottest and driest. The casual visitor
is most likely to see him crossing a road or racing with a
car. But one may see him also in the wildest wilds, either
on the desert flats or high up in the desert canyons where
he strides along over rocks and between shrubs. Indeed,
one may see him almost anywhere below the level where
desert gives way to pines or aspen.

He will come into your patio if you are discreet. Taken
young from the nest, he will make a pet, and one writer
describes a tame individual who for years roosted on top
a wall clock in a living room, sleeping quietly through
evening parties unless a visitor chose to occupy the chair
just below his perch, in which case he would wake up,
descend upon the intruder, and drive him away. But the
road runner is not one who needs either the human inhabitant or anything which human beings have introduced.
Not only his food but everything else he wants is amply
supplied in his chosen environment. He usually builds his
sketchy nest out of twigs from the most abundant tree, the
mesquite. He places it frequently in a cholla, the wicked-
est of the cacti upon whose murderous spines even snakes
are sometimes found fatally impaled. He feeds his young
as he feeds himself, upon the reptiles which inhabit the
same areas which he does. And because they are juicy,
neither he nor his young are as dependent upon the hard-
to-find water as the seed-eating birds who must sometimes
make long trips to get it.

Yet all the road runner's peculiarities represent things learned, and learned rather recently as a biologist understands "recent." He is not a creature who happened to have certain characteristics and habits and who therefore survived here. This is a region he moved into and he was once very different. As a matter of fact, so the ornithologists tell us, he is actually a cuckoo, although no one would ever guess it without studying his anatomy. Outwardly, there is nothing to suggest the European cuckoo of reprehensible domestic morals or, for that matter, the American cuckoo or "rain crow" whose mournful note is familiar over almost the entire United States and part of Canada—not excluding the wooded oases of Arizona itself. That cuckoo flies, perches, sings and eats conventional bird food. He lives only where conditions are suited to his habits. But one of his not too distant relatives must have moved into the desert—slowly, no doubt—and made himself so much at home there that by now he is a cuckoo only to those who can read the esoteric evidences of his anatomical structure.

Despite all this, it must be confessed that not everybody loves the road runner. Nothing is so likely to make an animal unpopular as a tendency to eat things which we ourselves would like to eat. And the road runner is guilty of just this wickedness. He is accused, no doubt justly, of varying his diet with an occasional egg of the Gambel's quail, or even with an occasional baby quail itself. Sportsmen are afraid that this reduces somewhat the number they will be able to kill in their own more efficient way and so, naturally, they feel that the road runner should be eliminated.

To others it seems that a creature who so triumphantly

demonstrates how to live in the desert ought to be regarded with sympathetic interest by those who are trying
to do the same thing. He and the quail have got along
together for quite a long time. Neither seems likely to
eliminate the other. Man, on the other hand, may very
easily eliminate both. It is the kind of thing he is best at.

THREE

strange forest

IN THE PLANT WORLD THE ROAD RUNNER'S OPPOSITE NUM-
ber is certainly the cactus. To most people—and quite
properly—it is the desert plant par excellence. Many kinds
are, like the road runner, at home in the desert and nowhere else. Like the road runner also they belong to a
family of pioneers which moved into arid America and
changed itself radically to meet the new conditions. Most
of the cuckoo tribe live by following other habits in other
environments. The relatives of the desert cacti do the same.

Members of the Sonoran branch of the family come in all
shapes and sizes from tiny two-inch pincushions full of pins

to the giant saguaro which towers sometimes seventy-five feet, weighs six or seven tons, and lives for as much as two hundred years. Some eleven sorts of cactus have been found only in Arizona, other kinds are more widespread. But they all have the same general characteristics and employ very similar devices in their determination to make a good best of desert living.

Most have the succulent stems which store water, when they can get it, to be saved for a non-rainy day—or month, or even year. Leaves are vestigial or completely absent because too much moisture would evaporate from them, and the stems are green with chlorophyll so that they can perform the functions of leaves. These stems are also often coated with wax to economize water still further and usually they are provided with formidable spines—partly to discourage animals which would be only too glad to use the succulence for their own purposes, partly because spines limit the free circulation of the hot, desiccating atmosphere, perhaps also because they provide broken shade to the surface of the plant.

All these devices have been independently invented by other plant families which also moved into the desert. Succulence, waxy coatings, and reduced or absent leaves are common. To the layman, indeed, any plant which exhibits all these characteristics is commonly called "a cactus," though he is often wrong because the true cactus is a member of a family strongly marked in other ways. That graceful spray of ten-foot wands tipped with flame-colored flowers and called ocotillo is no more a cactus because it has spines and bears no leaves except during wet weather than a butterfly is a bird because it has wings.

In the case of the butterfly and the bird two quite different creatures learned to fly by inventing wings. In the case of the ocotillo and the cactus two different kinds of plants discovered the same methods of economizing on water. Nevertheless, true cacti are common enough and a number of species are growing within a few feet of my door. The why and wherefore of their diverse shapes and habits is an interesting subject, but at the moment we are concerned rather with the general methods by which cacti have learned to live in the desert.

The question might be asked of any one of a dozen sorts but we may as well address it to the giant saguaro. For one thing, it is in many ways among the most remarkable of all. For another, not even the most casual visitor to the region where it grows can have failed to be aware that it is unlike anything to be seen elsewhere. There must be few Americans who are not at least vaguely familiar with drawings or paintings or photographs of the saguaro towering starkly over the desert and stretching out its grotesquely extended arms. As a matter of fact, artists and cartoonists have established it as a conventional symbol of location. When you see a saguaro that means, "Scene: The Desert" just as the Eiffel Tower means "Paris" or The Public Library lions mean "New York." Actually it has been employed far too widely for even reasonable accuracy. To many artists it seems to mean not only "desert" but "any desert," though the truth is that the saguaro's range is extraordinarily limited. There are some in northern Mexico; there are also a very few in California just across the Colorado River from Arizona. But, except for these, there are no others anywhere in the

world and the symbol ought to mean not "desert" but "the
Sonoran Desert of southwestern Arizona and northern
Mexico." To the traveler approaching from the east or
the north, the first sight of a saguaro standing sentinel is
the announcement, "I have arrived."

Under the special conditions prevailing where it flourishes best—loose rocky soil, low rainfall and high temperature—no other growth achieves such a height or such
a bulk. Inevitably the saguaro suggests some strange kind
of tree, not a succulent plant, and its weight is tremendous.
As we said a few minutes ago it may tower fifty feet and
may weigh 12,000 pounds. Indeed, fully grown plants are
quite commonly not much smaller. Yet they are obviously, in everything except size, very much like other
members of the sometimes quite modest cereus subgroup
of the cacti. The waxy green skin is tender; the flesh is
pulpy and moist, though the moisture contained is too
bitter to drink. In spring when a little circle of white
flowers opens at the tip of one or more of the arms, the
flowers are unmistakably cactus flowers. When the red
fruits follow they look like many other cactus fruits, even
very much like the familiar prickly pear sometimes sold
in fruit stores.

Yet everything about the saguaro is somehow odd. The
seeds, like most cactus seeds, are tiny. The disproportion
between the acorn and the oak is not nearly so great. And
they grow with extraordinary slowness. After two or three
years a seedling is only a few millimeters high; after ten
years, less than an inch. From then on the rate of growth
is variable, but a three-foot specimen may be twenty to
fifty years old. In middle age (or shall we say adolescence)
it will grow faster, but it will take about a century to

reach maturity, after which an individual may have another hundred years to live. Planting a tree is often taken as a symbol of the farseeing and the unselfish. One puts an acorn in the ground with a certain sense of demonstrating both faith in and concern for a future other than one's own. But if anyone ever planted a saguaro for the sake of future generations, he was carrying such faith and such concern to fantastic limits.

Yet in favorable areas the saguaros form veritable forests, thousands of specimens covering hundreds of acres grow almost as close together as giant trees do. Obviously the saguaro is extremely well suited to what it is suited to. There is no suggestion that it would prefer any other environment. Indeed, the fact that it is so restricted in its distribution, that it does not tolerate introduction into other parts of the world, is proof enough how perfectly it has adapted itself. What makes it so fit to live just here?

The most uninstructed visitor who saw a forest of these giants for the first time would almost certainly assume that their roots go very deep down. If he happened to know something about the habits of certain other desert plants —how, for example, a yucca no more than six or eight feet high may send a root forty feet below the surface in search of water—he would probably suppose that the saguaro must reach half the way to China. But he couldn't be more wrong. The taproot of a huge specimen is seldom more than three feet long and seems ridiculously inadequate. As a matter of fact the saguaro is so insecurely anchored that it often meets its end by being blown over in a storm, and wanton horsemen have been known to destroy in a few moments a century of slow living with a tug upon a lasso.

Yet there is method in the saguaro's seeming madness. It does not go deep for water because where it grows there usually isn't any. In fact its preferred areas are those buried under the loose rocky detritus of disintegrating mountains and therefore the very ones which are the despair of the well digger. But the saguaro has learned that when the occasional torrential rains do come, the water does not run off as quickly as it does on the hard-backed flats because it sinks a few inches into the rocky soil. And while the saguaro was learning that, it was also learning how to take advantage of the fact. It sends out a network of lateral roots only eight to twenty inches below the surface but as much as ninety feet in length, so that the great trunk rises from the center of a sort of huge disk just below the surface.

Thanks to this arrangement it is ready to take full advantage of the occasional periods when these roots are bathed in water. Moreover the trunk is longitudinally accordion-pleated and as moisture is absorbed the pleats unfold. As much as a ton may be absorbed after a single downpour and the supply, carefully hoarded, can last if necessary for a full year.

In fact the saguaro cannot live where rains are frequent because, for one thing, it may take up so much water as to burst itself open. Even when growing under ideal conditions, it may have a moisture content of from seventy-five to ninety-five percent of its green weight. In a saguaro forest the large plants are usually fifteen or twenty feet apart, because each needs a considerable area from which

to draw water, and the mature specimens are those
which have successfully defended the plot of ground to
which a seedling staked a claim perhaps a century ago. In
a deciduous forest the contest between individuals is literally for a place in the sun. Where the saguaro grows there
is enough of that for everybody. But every individual
must protect his water rights in his own area.

For all the soft succulence of the saguaro's trunk, for
all the fact that it is not, like a tree, predominantly woody,
there is nothing weak about its structure. It may sway
in the wind like an oak or an elm; in a storm, branching
"arms" may sometimes break off, or the whole may be uprooted. But the massive trunk is surprisingly strong. Indeed, when you realize that the flesh beneath the waxy
skin is soft and pulpy, it is astonishingly so.

Examine the skeleton of a dead specimen lying on the
desert and the mystery is explained. The soft part decayed
rapidly but there remained the almost indestructible
woody "ribs," each as long as the saguaro was high. Among
the many remarkable discoveries of this cactus was the
discovery of the principle of "reinforcement" which man
now takes advantage of when he embeds steel rods in his
concrete walls. The center of the saguaro is pulpy and
so is the outer flesh. But imbedded in this pulp is a cylin-
der of closely placed rods which give the whole a flexible
strength. Since the time before history, Pima and Papago
Indians living in the saguaro country have used these
rods to construct wooden shelters which must be as immune to decay as cypress.

In another way also, the saguaro finds that its ability to
produce either pulpy or extraordinarily hard tissue comes
in handy. It is very much subject to the attack of wood-

peckers. In fact one species of the latter, the gilded flicker, seldom nests in anything except a hole which it has excavated in the saguaro, and its range is almost coextensive with that of the giant cactus. Moreover, this particular bird insists upon digging a new home ever so often, leaving abandoned dwellings to be used by quite a few other species of nesting birds—by cactus wrens, elf owls and others, even sometimes, as I have happened to observe, by honeybees who have left their man-made hive. The result of all this is that there are very few mature saguaros which do not have from one to a dozen cavities in their trunks. But the saguaro handles this situation very successfully. The wound inflicted by the flicker is quickly sealed off by a layer of extraordinarily tough scar-tissue. Not infrequently one finds among the bleached ribs of some long dead saguaro a curious boot-shaped receptacle which represents the lining of a flicker's nest. The Sonoran Desert must be one of the few places in the world where one may come home from a walk carrying a hole—and a very durable one at that.

For plants which grow only in one or more isolated and very restricted areas the botanists have a word: "endemic." Endemics contrast most sharply with "cosmopolitans" which sometimes almost circle the globe, somewhat less sharply with other species or genera which cover large areas without being actually cosmopolitan. But there are few species whose endemism is more striking than that of the saguaro which is limited to this one small area. And there are few if any endemics which are so striking a feature of the one region where they are at home.

Both cosmopolitanism and endemism present problems

for the evolutionist and the plant geographer. How did the cosmopolitans spread from, say, Africa to South America? Why haven't those endemics which are found only in one place set forth to colonize others? How did those which exist in several widely separated but restricted areas come to have this "discontinuous distribution"?

The answers to those questions when either found or guessed at are various. Obviously a plant species or genus can't migrate past barriers which it cannot cross. A plant adapted, for instance, to desert conditions obviously can't get to another desert thousands of miles away across a damp, humid stretch any more than a moisture-loving plant can cross a desert from one moist region to another. If, as happens to be the case, there are very closely related cosmopolitan genera in Africa and in South America, they must have made their way from one continent to another via some land connections either now or once existing. No less obviously, if endemics are "discontinuously distributed" in several small, widely separate areas, that presents a different problem. And in some cases at least they probably represent "relicts"—surviving patches of some once large continuous distribution.

All this is part of a very large and complicated subject into which we need not try to enter very deeply. But once one has turned from astonishment at the saguaro as an individual to contemplate the fact that it is not to be found anywhere except in this one region where it is so very abundant indeed, one cannot help wondering why that should be. Were there ever saguaros anywhere else? Are they "relicts" or did they first develop here and never get any further?

Such questions cannot be answered fully and positively

but some very probable guesses can be made. No remains of a saguaro, fossil or otherwise, have ever been found except in this region. By itself that is not very strong evidence because fossil cacti of any kind are almost unknown. But certain other facts can be added. The cactus is an American family so there can't be much doubt that the saguaro originated in this hemisphere. It is so highly specialized that it will not flourish except under the very special conditions which it finds in this one kind of desert. If it ever colonized a larger area, it must have been one which was at that time almost precisely what the Sonoran Desert is now. And for all these reasons it seems a fairly safe guess that there never were any saguaros in any place very far from where they are now found.

Look again, therefore, at any one of the thousands to be seen in southern Arizona. Probably nowhere else was one ever seen. They represent about as close an approximation to a "special creation" as one is likely to find. They certainly look improbable, and in a sense they were improbable—until, for some reason which evolutionists don't even pretend to understand fully, an organism's ability to vary produced at last this strange plant perfectly adapted to the narrowly defined conditions which existed right here. The first known mention of the saguaro is said to be in 1540. Surely the botanical Cortez who first saw it must have felt "a wild surmise."

Nowadays we are all too familiar with the sad fact that many interesting plants and many interesting animals are "near extinction." Perhaps most people don't care but at least there are some who do. Like Thoreau they may say— and have even stronger reasons than he had for saying it—"I seek acquaintance with Nature . . . I take infinite pains to know all the phenomena of the spring, for instance, thinking that I have here the entire poem, and then to my chagrin, I hear that it is but an imperfect copy that I possess and have read, that my ancestors have torn out many of the first leaves and grandest passages, and mutilated it in many places."

For the immediate present, however, the saguaro insists upon being paradoxical in still another respect. In all probability there are now, or at least were quite recently, more saguaros in southern Arizona than there ever were before. The primeval forest of giant cacti which the first white man saw was probably neither as thick nor as imposing as the one you and I can see today!

Careful study of the composition of the existing forests seems to demonstrate conclusively that they experienced a rather short period of unusual prosperity not so very long ago, that neither before nor since that time did the species ever reproduce itself so abundantly or so vigorously. This does not mean that young saguaros are not even at this moment moving slowly through the stages of their growth. One may find them a few inches or a few feet high, usually in the shade of some bush or some cactus of a different species which shaded them from the too fierce sun during their earliest years. But from the proportion of existing specimens of approximately the same age, it seems clear that about two hundred years ago conditions were more nearly perfect than they were before or have been since. Nowadays, so it is estimated, only about one out of every 275,000 seeds reaches maturity. Once the proportion must, for reasons not definitely known, have been much greater. And since the saguaro is so demanding a plant, even though what it demands is not what most other plants would, the situation is not really surprising. A very slight change in temperature, amount of rainfall, or any one of a number of other things, would no doubt react sharply upon it.

Already the heyday is past. As old specimens die there are fewer new ones to take their place. Gradually the forests are thinning out and though measures are being taken to protect so unique an example of the wonders of creation, it seems likely enough that the saguaro is doomed, at least sometime during the centuries to come. That also, however, is not too surprising. Ecologists have long recognized the fact that too high a degree of specialization is usually fatal to a species whether it be plant or animal. The more adaptable kinds roll with the punches when conditions change. But no matter how perfectly a plant or animal may be suited to some very narrow range of conditions, it is almost certain to be helpless when either man or the slow evolution of the earth's surface changes those conditions only slightly.

Thus the great ivory billed woodpecker will almost certainly be extinct in a few years if it is not extinct already. It must have great forests with many dead trees. Great forests are shrinking and even in those that remain, good forestry which requires the removal of dead wood is bad forestry for the ivory bill. Meanwhile the very adaptable English sparrow survived even the disappearance of the horse and, according to reliable report, has in places taken to haunting filling stations for the purpose of picking insects from the radiators of the very automobiles which drove the horse, its former supplier, from the roads.

One wonders what will happen to the gilded flicker.

He is very nearly what the ornithologists call an "obligate" of the saguaro, i.e., a species which cannot live except where the saguaro does. But it is said that he does not refuse absolutely to nest in any hole except one which he has excavated in the giant cactus. Perhaps that concession will save him, as a similar one saved (or perhaps profited) the chimney swift of the East when he moved from caves into the more numerous man-made chimneys.

In any event, one thing seems pretty certain. Those of us who admire the saguaro arrived just in the nick of time. A few centuries ago would have been too soon. A few centuries hence would probably be too late.

F O U R

how they got that way

ONCE, A VERY LONG TIME AGO, DINOSAURS LUMBERED OVER parts of what is now Arizona and, departing, left behind them footprints in the muds of time. Occasionally the mud hardened into stone and the prints are pointed out to visitors. Concerning them a pleasant story is told.

"Them footprints," said a guide, "is four hundred million and four years old." "But how can you be so precise as all that?" "Well, (apologetically) of course I don't really know nothing about it myself. But when I came they told me they was four hundred million years old. And I been here four years."

This tale is one it is well to bear in mind when discussing either geology or evolution. Even the most confident scientists admit that they can't "be so precise as all that." In fact they much prefer to talk about the relative age of either rocks or fossils rather than to assign dates, and of course amateurs have even better reason to be cautious. But it is impossible to talk about cuckoos which turned into road runners and plants which lost their leaves without beginning to wonder when they did it.

How long ago did the road runner colonize the desert and the cactus begin to live there? How long, for that matter, has there been a desert in this region for them to colonize? None of these questions can be answered as definitely as students of rocks, or plants, or animals would like to answer them, but they are not totally unanswerable either. And we might as well start with the desert itself.

Many parts of the earth have been desert-like at many different periods. During at least part of Paleozoic times (and that means hundreds of millions of years ago) much of New York and Pennsylvania, for example, was a desert, though there were certainly no road runners or cacti there because that was a long long time before there were any birds or any flowering plants of any kind. And the region around New York City was to be buried under the ice at least twice between then and now.

Similarly, the Southwest also has had its ups and downs, literally as well as figuratively. About the time when New York and Pennsylvania were desert, spreading seas were lapping about the region of Tucson, as sedimentary rocks in what are now the Santa Rita and the Tucson Mountains show. Later deposits, formed in other parts of Arizona, indicate that highly arid conditions prevailed there then.

Nevertheless, and still later, toward the end of the Mesozoic era, or say a hundred million years ago, most of what
is now the Rocky Mountain region was part of a great
seaway five hundred to a thousand miles wide, stretching
from the Gulf of Mexico to the arctic, and covering parts
of New Mexico, Texas and eastern Arizona, so that much
of what is now arid was drowned in salt water then.

Presently the Rockies, the Sierra Nevadas, and the Cas-
cade Mountains appeared, cutting off, as they were lifted,
the moist winds blowing in from the Pacific. Hence the
Great Basin area of Utah was soon very dry and the
Great Plains semi-arid. But until the mountain ranges
reached their greatest height, their eastern flanks were
probably warmer and moister than they are now. And as
for the Sonoran Desert, it is probably relatively recent,
though the Sonoran has been something like what it now
is since the Miocene, which means for approximately ten
million years.

The evidence indicates that the eastern or dry flanks of
the Andes were also very dry by then, and because close
relatives of some of our most characteristic desert plants
are found in South America, it is thought that they probably originated there. Moreover, the soil of the Sonoran
Desert floor is much younger than the mountains which
surround it, because it is a thick layer of detritus washed
down from these same mountains as they have weathered
away and it now fills the once deeper valleys. In places
it is at least 1800 feet thick, as we know from the fact
that well drillers in the Tucson area have failed to find
rock even at that depth. Even now the desert is changing—in some respects rapidly, because of what man has
done to it since he set cattle and sheep to grazing and

overgrazing the desert vegetation, in others slowly, because nature herself does not stand still.

On the other hand, new as the desert is in terms of geology and relatively new as it is in terms of its flora and fauna, it is still very ancient from man's own standpoint. It seems to be quite definitely established that Indians were already inhabiting some parts of the Southwest as much as ten thousand years ago, and if any of them had already got to southern Arizona, they must have found it not too unlike what it is today, though some of the vegetation was probably less sparse. But "ten thousand years ago" really is "today" so far as the story of evolution is concerned. Long before that, European man had reached a stage of mental development which made his skull nearly identical with that of us moderns. Long before that a road runner, scarcely if at all distinguishable from those now rejoicing in the desert and dry coastal areas, had fallen into the famous tar pits near Los Angeles where its bones remained until they were dug up a few years ago.

Since the cactus is even stranger as a plant than the road runner is as a bird, it is perhaps of the cactus that we had better ask, diffidently but more specifically, the questions proposed a few paragraphs back. "How and when did you get here? Where did you come from? What were your ancestors like? By what stages did you adapt yourself so admirably to the very special conditions you found in the southwestern deserts?"

At least a partial answer can be given to these questions, though the answers have to be based not on geological evidence but upon a study of the living members of the cactus family. Some of them grow in regions only slightly arid and some of those which do so, do not look at all like what we think of when we hear the word "cactus." They have quite ordinary leaves and stems. In fact they are not very unusual in appearance. And the assumption is that it was some such quite orthodox member of an orthodox family which learned to live with less and less water as it turned itself into a desert species.

Now, at some of these statements the layman may well bristle. "Why on earth," he may ask, "do you tell me that the ocotillo—which has thorns, green stems, and only small temporary leaves—is not a cactus, while some quite ordinary-looking plant which lives in a reasonably damp environment is? Why wouldn't it be more sensible to say that the ocotillo and the cactus are alike, that they descended from some common ancestor which was, and perhaps always had been, desert dwelling and cactus-like?"

The answer to that protest is very much like the answer to the question, "Why call the road runner a cuckoo?" You call him that because of certain fundamental anatomical characteristics which, as we know from fossil and other evidence, change much more slowly than the superficial peculiarities which make him seem at first glance uncuckoo-like.

All botanists, whether they be students of the living species or of fossils, agree that the anatomy of the flower is one of the more stable characteristics of a plant group. Classification is based upon all the characteristics of a plant, and the flower structure and the obscure anatomy of all desert cacti are similar, while they are different from those of the ocotillo and other superficially similar plants. The tropical cactus of a moist environment may not look like its desert cousin, but its flower is much like theirs, while that of the ocotillo is different.

Of course it would be nice if we had a complete series of dated fossils which would illustrate the emergence in time of the relatively superficial characteristics of the desert cactus. In the case of various animals, such series do exist, notably in the case of the horse, whose evolution was illustrated quite early in the study of evolution and whose gradual loss of toes can be neatly demonstrated in the successive cases of a museum. Unfortunately, however, nothing of the sort is possible in the case of the cacti.

In the first place the whole order of flowering plants may have evolved rather late. In the second place deserts are not very favorable to the preservation of fossils, which occur most abundantly in what were once marshes or shallow seas. As a matter of fact, it is sometimes said that there are *no* fossil cacti and that therefore they must be very recent indeed. But this evidence is purely negative and a decade or two ago what may be a fossilized prickly pear was discovered in southern Utah embedded in deposits of the Eocene age. If it really is a prickly pear, then a cactus very like a modern one must have developed during an epoch which, according to the latest evidence, must be placed at least forty million years ago.

It is not even certain whether the drought-resisting devices were developed by plants growing in a region which gradually dried up, or whether they were developed as the plants increased their range into more and more arid regions. But if, by chance, the place where the one fossil of a prickly pear was found is the place where it developed its peculiarities, then it seems likely that the process was one of adjustment to a changing climate because, so the geologists say, the Great Basin section of Utah became drier and drier as the Eocene was succeeded by the Miocene, and by that epoch it may have been as dry as Death Valley is today. At least the best guess, based upon what evidence is available, seems to be that the cactus from Utah first learned somewhere how to survive dry seasons of the year between relatively wet ones and that then, having developed methods of saving water for a part of the year, it was finally able to survive almost continuous drought. And it might have done this right in Utah, since it seems pretty certain that this very region where the Eocene cactus was growing was a region which had become arid all the year around by the time it entered the next geological epoch.

By way of compensation for the paucity of fossil evidence bearing on the evolution of the cactus, there is something we do have: a rather remarkably complete series of *living* forms which illustrate very neatly many of the steps by which the not-at-all-cactus-like ancestor probably took on, one by one, the distinguishing characteristics of the most peculiar and specialized kinds. The eohippus or "dawn horse" is extinct. To illustrate his evolution we have only the fossils. In the case of the cactus the situation is exactly reversed. A plant probably similar to the "dawn cactus" is still growing in South America.

Perhaps just because cacti are so odd, so unlike what we expect a plant to be, they have been made the subject of exhaustive study. In the great four-volume work by Britton and Rose the living sorts are magnificently illustrated. In Berger's *Die Entwicklungslinien der Kakteen* the probable lines of development are exhaustively studied. Instead of the museum case showing the skeletons of successive horses, it is perfectly possible for a botanical garden to exhibit, alive and growing, the unspecialized ancestor and the most highly specialized desert species as well as many successive stages in between.

An interesting fact about the family and one which raises other questions is this: it seems to belong exclusively to the Western Hemisphere. With the possible exception of one peculiar species which may be native to Africa, all of the perhaps eight hundred kinds of cacti grow naturally only on our side of the world. On the other hand, many, many plant families are "cosmopolitan." You may, that is to say, find them growing as natives on several of the widely separated continents. But the cactus, unless one counts the single dubiously African species, are all American. If they ever grew naturally on any other continent they must have become extinct long ago.

This is by no means to say that they won't grow anywhere else if given a chance. Once they were taken to Africa, to Italy and the Holy Land by the hand of man, they flourished there. So, too, did they flourish in Australia. As a matter of fact, when the prickly pear was incautiously introduced there, it liked conditions so well that it became a disastrous pest. Believed to have been introduced in 1839 as one plant in a flowerpot, it began to get out of hand about thirty years later. By 1900 it had taken over some ten million acres; by 1920 it dominated sixty million; and it was estimated to be rendering land useless at the rate of a million acres a year. Finally it was brought under control only after large sums and great effort had been expended.

This should convince the most skeptical that if cacti

did not exist in a wild state anywhere outside the Western Hemisphere, it was not because they did not like it anywhere else.

Neither can it be because only in America did climatic conditions or changes capable of developing drought-resisting plants occur. As a matter of fact, many different plant families in many parts of the world did develop the special features of desert dwelling plants so that the casual layman would unhesitatingly call them cacti. There are succulent mulberries in Australia and Africa, succulent passion flowers in Africa and, on one of the islands of the Indian Ocean, there is a succulent member of the gourd family which develops a sixteen-foot trunk like an inverted carrot.

Or suppose we take the case of the milkweeds. Nearly everybody who has paid any attention to our native plants in either the wet or dry regions is familiar with one or another member of this family. In our deserts there are several species and some of them have the narrow, hard, dry leaves characteristic of so many plants growing in dry air. Visitors from elsewhere must often have been surprised to see a cluster of unmistakable milkweed flowers topping a plant which looks, at first sight, as though it were clothed in pine needles. Nevertheless, no Arizona species has a succulent, water-storing stem or looks anything like a cactus. Yet in Africa and also in Asia there are related plants which, though not spiny, look a good deal like cacti. They are nearly leafless and they store moisture in their stems.

But perhaps the most interesting case of all is that of the African members of the cosmopolitan Euphorbia family, of which the Arizona limber bush is a characteristic representative. They independently developed almost precisely the devices which seem typical of the cacti, though no North American species of Euphorbia ever did. Some of the African sorts have thick, columnar, leafless stems, waxy coatings and defensive spines, all of which make them look so cactus-like that even an amateur who had got beyond the stage of calling an ocotillo a cactus might be forgiven if he took it for granted that at least these African Euphorbias really were cacti. But they are not. Their flowers are totally different from cactus flowers, and they have the thick milky juice which is not characteristic of the cacti but is characteristic of the Euphorbia family as a whole and is, indeed, responsible for the utility of the economically most valuable members of the family—namely the rubber plants.

If then, the fact that the true cacti are all American does not mean that cacti cannot live anywhere else and does not mean that only in America did plants develop drought-resisting devices similar to the cactus, then what on earth does it mean?

No one can answer that question with absolute finality, but what it probably does mean is that the cactus family not only began in America, but began quite recently— as such things go; much more recently than, for example, the milkweeds and the Euphorbias. And the reason for this deduction is not hard to understand.

Obviously the cosmopolitan families migrated somehow from one continent to another. As early as the days of Darwin and Wallace it was assumed that such families were older than the "endemic" which, in some cases at least, were endemic simply because they did not arise until after the routes along which the other groups had spread were closed in one way or another. The classic example of a similar phenomenon in the animal world is the nearly complete absence of native mammals in Australia despite the fact that they are native to every other continent. Obviously their ancestors, the marsupials, had got to Australia across some bridge which had disappeared before the marsupial stock had evolved true mammalian form somewhere on one of the continents by then isolated from Australia.

No botanist would say today that every endemic family or genus is bound to be younger than any cosmopolitan one. It is not so simple as all that. For one thing the existence of "discontinuous distributions" (i.e., genera endemic in several widely separated regions) is sufficient to suggest that an endemic genus may sometimes be merely the relict of a cosmopolitan one which has become extinct except in a few places. But if a plant found in one place never did exist anywhere else, then it probably originated fairly recently and somewhere not too far from where it is now found. Something like that is probably (but only probably) the case with the cactus.

In any event, most would probably agree that this much may be said with a fair degree of assurance: the cactus originated, either in Mexico or South America, as a normal enough plant with slender stems and orthodox leaves like one member of the family (Pereskia) still growing in the West Indies and South America. That ancestral cactus may have been accustomed then to a fairly moist environment and it is in such an environment that it still flourishes. But from a remote period it has always been distinguished by the anatomical peculiarities of the family —notably by a certain floral structure and the presence of a unique organ called the areole from which spines are produced. Members of this family spread both northward and southward and somewhere, possibly in what is now one of the American deserts, they developed characteristics which enabled them to survive a long annual dry season. Then, when the slow lifting of mountains either in North or South America turned a seasonally dry climate into a perpetually arid region they were well on the way to their present ability to tolerate not only seasonal but almost continuous drought. If all our western mountains had always been where they are now, there might be no cactus here because the country would always have been too dry to permit the slow adaptation of the family to arid conditions. If, on the other hand, the mountains were not there now, then at least many of the kinds of cactus now decorating the landscape would not be there either, because the climate would be too moist for them.

What it all comes down to is this: the casual visitor to the desert may not always be sure what is a cactus and what is not. But he is quite right when he thinks of cacti as the most characteristic plants of the region. Few others have managed so successfully to make themselves so completely at home there. No compromises, no eludings, no picking out of damp spots for the cactus. When he came to the desert he took possession of it. Like the road runner, he can say, as few other things can, "Veni, vidi, vici."

F I V E

he was there before Coronado

ACCORDING TO AN ANCIENT AND ANONYMOUS JOCOSITY THE bravest man who ever lived must have been the first to eat an oyster—alive.

A soberer judgment might want to make a case for that equally forgotten hero of paleolithic times who first domesticated fire. It must have been one of the first of his home-building achievements, but no wolf destined to turn into a dog and no buffalo destined to become a cow can possibly have seemed one-tenth so dangerous as devouring flame. Early man, like every other animal, must have long been accustomed to flee from it in abject terror. We shall never know what Prometheus first dared snatch a bit from some forest fire or some erupting volcano. But when he put it down in the middle of the domestic circle he must have said, "This I can tame and use."

Long before even his day, courage of some sort must have been a characteristic of living things and even the tamer of fire was not the first hero. Perhaps the first and greatest of all was whatever little blob of jelly—not yet either plant or animal but a little of both—first consented to take on the responsibility of being alive at all. And surely the second greatest was that plant or animal which first dared leave the water where, ever since the very dawn of creation, every other organism before it had been born and died. Men are talking now about journeys to the moon or to Mars, but neither is more unsuited to human life than the bare earth was to the first creatures who risked it.

For millions of years only the submerged areas of the earth had been habitable. It was in water that the first hypothetical one-celled creatures, too insubstantial to leave fossil remains, must have been generated. None ventured out of it during millions of years while stony skeletons were evolved and became the earliest sure evidence of life in some of the oldest rocks. In water also stayed all the wormlike and squidlike and shrimplike creatures which represented, in their day, the highest development of life. Meanwhile, during the major part of the earth's history, during considerably more than half the time since life began, all dry land was desert to a degree almost inconceivable—without soil of any kind, as bare as the moon, and subject to no changes except those produced by geological forces. Volcanoes flowed and mountains heaved. Rain falling on an earth without any plant cover to protect it washed cruel gullies as remorselessly as they are cut in the most unqualified "bad lands" of today. Had any creature of that time been capable of thought, life in any medium other than water would have seemed as fantastic as life without an atmosphere would seem to us.

Then at some time, geologists say it was probably something like three hundred million years ago, the first living thing dared to expose itself temporarily to the deadly air. If it was an animal, as some think most probable, then it must have rushed back (or perhaps ducked back) before the gills through which it breathed could dry out. It could hardly have done much more during many thousands of years after the first bold venture, because it could not actually live beyond easy reach of water until its whole anatomy and physiology had undergone fundamental changes. But patience is a quality which the universe seems never to have lacked (until man came along) and it was always the animal which broke most rashly with all previous tradition, which presently became the most highly developed and the most competent—as well as the least patient.

So far as I am concerned I see no reason to apologize for calling that animal a "hero" or for referring to his "courage." Such terms can have no real meaning except in connection with something which is alive and when we talk about "the suffering earth" or the "nobility" of a mountain range we are merely using a figure of speech. But it is hard to say just where reality begins or to decide just which animal or even which plant is still too simple to be capable of something genuinely analogous to daring and courage. If these virtues are real in man, then they are real because they began to be so as soon as there was anything in the universe which could defy law and habit by risking something which had never been done before.

Few of us are so committed to a merely mechanical behaviorism that we would refuse to call brave and adventurous the first human pioneers who came to live in the American West. So in their own way were the plants and animals who had preceded them there. And so, *a fortiori,* were those far back in time who first dared learn how to adapt themselves to that desert which all dry land then was. If daring to do what our intelligence recognizes as dangerous constitutes "courage," then the animal who similarly rejects the imperatives of its instinct is exhibiting a virtue at least analogous, and so, in some still dimmer fashion, is the simplest creature, animal or even vegetable, which refuses to obey its long established reflexes. The whole course of evolution is directed by just such courageous acts. It must have its countless unremembered heroes who created diversity by daring to do what no member of its species had ever done before.

Most scientists, I am well aware, would object strenuously to any such line of reasoning. But then many scientists are firmly convinced that in man himself there is also no such thing as either daring or courage as distinguished from a reflex, congenital or conditioned. And perhaps that conclusion is inevitable if you begin by denying their reality to all creatures "lower" than man. If every other animal is a machine then why shouldn't human beings be machines also. And if to speak of the "courage" of some very lowly creature is to indulge in exaggeration, it is at least an exaggeration opposite and corrective to a more usual one.

Is it possible, one may ask, to guess at the identity of the first great pioneer and radical who came to dry land? Or is it, like the song the Sirens sang, "beyond all conjecture?" Does he have a name and can we honor him by saying, "But for you and your enterprise I might still be a fish?" At least our own direct amphibious ancestors came to land only because that pioneer's descendants were there to be eaten!

Well, if the paleontologists are right—and their evidence seems pretty good—we can answer this question. As a matter of fact, I met only the day before yesterday one of the almost unchanged relatives of the first air-breathing creatures, and he did not seem especially proud. He crawled on eight legs out from under a board in my storeroom and I confess that, though I do not do such things lightly, I put my foot upon him. Before he was crushed into nothing he was about two inches long and pale straw in color. He carried two pinchers before him and over his back he carried a long tail with a sting at its end. He was, in short, one of the least popular of desert dwellers—a scorpion.

Finding out about one's ancestors, especially correlative ones, is often a risky business and perhaps most people would rather not know how much all of us are indebted to this rather unattractive creature. But so far as geologists can tell from the fossils they study and date, the first animal actually capable of breathing air was not only a member of the scorpion kind but amazingly like the one we step on when we find him.

To even the most uninstructed eye a scorpion fossilized during the Silurian or Devonian epoch—say something like three hundred million years ago—is unmistakably a scorpion. If one of them were to come to life again and crawl out of his stone sarcophagus into your desert patio, you would not be particularly surprised by his appearance unless you happened to be a biologist especially devoted to the study of that group of animals called arachnids to which the scorpion belongs. There are several species now common hereabout—some, like the victim of my brutality, only two inches long and some several times that length. A three hundred million year old specimen would look to the casual eye like merely a sort one had not happened to see before and not much more different from the familiar kinds than they are from one another.

In the highly improbable event that a living dinosaur should be found in some African or South American hiding place, it would create quite a stir in even the popular press and any big-game hunter would count it a high distinction to shoot one. Yet anyone who happens to live in one of the many parts of the earth where scorpions abound can have the privilege of stepping upon a creature who has been going about his business (such as it is) far longer than any dinosaur went about dinosaur business. As a matter of fact, scorpions put in their appearance more years before the first dinosaur than have slipped away since the last known dinosaur decided that he and his kind had had their day.

The horseshoe crab and the gingko tree are sometimes called "living fossils," and the epithet has more recently been applied to that strange fish known as Latimeria which was taken not many years ago off the coast of Africa in spite of the fact that it, as well as all its immediate relatives, was supposed to have become extinct a very long time ago. Yet no sort of fish is much older than the scorpion, and the horseshoe crab is not as nearly like any very ancient form as the scorpion in my storeroom is like his Silurian ancestor. He may not be much to look at, but the least we can do is to regard him in the spirit of the naturalist Sutherland when he contemplated the living members of a tribe somewhat less ancient than the scorpions: "If the test of nobility is antiquity of family, then the cockroach that hides behind the kitchen sink is the true aristocrat. He does not date back merely to the three brothers who came over in 1640 or to William the Conqueror. Wherever there have been great epoch-making movements of people he has been with them heart and soul. . . . Since ever a ship turned a foamy furrow in the sea he has been a passenger, not a paying one certainly but still a passenger. But man himself is but a creature of the last twenty minutes or so compared with the cockroach, for, from its crevice by the kitchen sink, it can point its antennae to the coal in the hod and say: 'When that was being made my family was already well established.'" Scorpions have never been as closely associated with man as the cockroach, but they may not consider that anything to be ashamed of and on the score of antiquity they have a right to snub the cockroaches as upstarts, relatively speaking at least.

It may seem odd that they have hung on so long while changing so little. It may seem even odder that they should be found in deserts despite the fact that they are so similar to the scorpions which had recently left the water. But they do not insist upon its being dry and some species will even tolerate a certain amount of cold. Though there are none in New England or in the Great Lakes region, they are found in the Alps and on our continent as far north as southern Canada. On the whole, however, they prefer warm climates and they have been in the Southwest for a long, long time. Tracks almost precisely like those made by a living species have been found in the Coconino sandstone which was laid down in Permian times or not more than a million or a million and a half years after scorpions took the first drastic step out of the water.

Most people today underestimate the intelligence and awareness of most creatures other than man because recent official science has often encouraged them to do so. But the scorpion is probably even dumber than he looks. At first sight you would have no reason to suppose that his senses were much less keen or his awareness much less dim than those of any common insect. But they are. By comparison even a beetle, to say nothing of a bee, an ant or a fly, is a miracle of alertness and competence. The life which I extinguished when I stepped on my specimen was about as dim as we can imagine life to be. The scorpion's brain stopped growing not long after he left the water and braininess had not got very far by then.

Neither his habits nor his character are very engaging even as such things go. The young—miniature replicas of their parents—are born alive and like the young of the wolf spider they clamber about on their mother's back until they are old enough to take care of themselves. But maternal solicitude is probably a rather large term to use in connection with the mother's tolerance, and at least until mating time comes around, scorpions do not seem to do anything very interesting. They skulk under bits of wood or stone and they sometimes choose to hide in shoes incautiously left in their neighborhood. I have never seen a scorpion outside captivity do anything more interesting than to nibble rather languidly at the body of a moth who had come to my light.

In fact, watching scorpions closely even in captivity does not provide much excitement most of the time. If two or three are kept together one sometimes absent-mindedly eats a companion but the cannibalism, which is usual, is probably nothing very deliberate. The poor things not only have a very rudimentary brain but also eyesight which is probably just keen enough to distinguish the dark corners where they hide from the bright light they avoid and too dim even to make them aware of movement. Probably they do not actually perceive anything they do not touch.

As one observer has put it, if you see two together then they are either making love or one of them is being eaten. Even anatomically the most interesting thing about scorpions is their curious way of breathing. Insects have, of course, no lungs. They have merely ramifying tubes open to the outside which permit the penetration of air into the body cavity. But scorpions, being even older than the insect tribe, have what are called book lungs—curious purselike organs which no insect possesses, though spiders, more nearly related to scorpions than to insects, often have both the insect's tubes or tracheae and the scorpion's book lungs. No doubt book lungs, which are a sort of air-breathing gills, were invented close to the water's edge.

So far as I know no detailed account of the mating habits of the Arizona species has ever been published, but in a creature which varies so little they are probably the same as those described in Henri Fabre's classic account of the kind which live in Provence and also, more recently, of a Philippine species. Male and female stand face to face with their tails raised and their stings touching. The male takes his partner by the claw and then backs away, leading her with him. This holding of hands in a sort of dance may last for more than an hour, after which the couple disappears under a stone or into some other recess, the male walking backward as he conducts his partner. This sounds almost romantic and it probably does involve a sort of courtship. But the holding of hands is also probably necessary because creatures which are deaf and almost blind can't afford to lose one another once happy accident has brought them together. And though human lovers have been known on occasion to call one another "good enough to eat," we are likely to be shocked when the female scorpion takes this extravagant metaphor literally, as she frequently does.

Even the scorpion's venom is said to be of some very ancient kind quite different from that of the serpent. And for once a creature commonly regarded as dangerous really is so to some slight extent. The largest kind are relatively innocuous and capable of giving, as I have been informed by a friend who knows from direct experience, nothing worse than a wasp sting. But two Arizona species, neither more than about two inches long, can be deadly to small children and may give even an adult several painful days in bed. Records kept at the Arizona State College over a period of nineteen years ending in 1948 charge them with causing sixty-four fatalities during that time, or more than four times as many as rattlesnakes can be blamed for. Naturalists get rather tired of insisting that few animals are dangerous at all and very few indeed anything like so dangerous as we like to imagine them, and it is almost a relief for them to be able to say: Scorpions really do sting, some species really are deadly to small children, and even adults should beware of them.

Even so, we tend to exaggerate their dangerousness both because we always do exaggerate such dangers and also perhaps because in the scorpion we recognize something terrifyingly ancient. Nevertheless, even the so-called deadly sort are deadly only to the very young or the very feeble and I myself have seen a healthy adult who had been stung by one ready to go back to his work after keeping fingers in ice water for an hour. By comparison with the automobile, they have very little effect upon the life expectancy of any inhabitant of the desert country. And though men have doubtless been killing them on sight at least since the earliest stone age, men must have found them impressive also, because Scorpio was put among the zodiacal constellations a very long time ago. And it is appropriate that this constellation, inconspicuous in the north, becomes very prominent in the summer sky above the desert.

So much, then, for this creature which, only a few pages back, I insisted upon endowing with "daring" and with "courage" because it ventured upon the land some three hundred millions of years ago. Judged even by the acuteness of its senses, much less by its intelligence, it belongs very low indeed in the hierarchy of life. What a long, long way it was from, say, the scorpion's eye—too primitive almost to deserve the name—to the eye of even so primitive an insect as the praying mantis. Yet the fact remains that between the scorpion and man himself the distance is not nearly so great as it is between the scorpion and anything which does not live at all. The difference between seeing, no matter how dimly, and not seeing at all is greater than the difference between the scorpion's vision and ours. It is easier to imagine how, given time enough, a scorpion could become a man than it is to imagine how sea water and mineral substances could have become a scorpion. Primitive as his eye is, it is indubitably an eye. Its owner can see with it—however dimly. And seeing itself is a process beyond comprehension. It involves awareness of some sort. Perhaps the difference between the scorpion's courage and what is possible for us is no greater than that between his eyesight and ours. Yet who would refuse to use the word "seeing" to describe what even a scorpion can do? Why should we not assume that his courage and ours are no less essentially, though remotely, the same?

Granting all this it is, however, still possible to wonder why this once so adventurous creature became so soon a very paragon of conservatism. As the first air-breather he may very well have been the remote ancestor of all the insects who were to proceed from originality to originality until they became capable of achievements which even man cannot wholly grasp. But this prototype of the insect himself continues to crawl upon the desert and to poison human beings with his ancient venom millions of years after almost all the other creatures which were even his near contemporaries gave up their effort to survive in their original forms. Like the horseshoe crab and the gingko tree, he should have become extinct eons ago. But he has changed even less than they and become one of the most striking examples not of evolution but of a refusal to evolve. Some of the irrational distaste and fear which the sight of him inspires in most people is partly the result of their dim half-realization that he comes down from a past too remote not to suggest unimaginable horrors. He is a living reminder of "the dark and backward abysm of time" and, like the earliest myths of the human race, he suggests the monstrous beginnings of instinct and mind and emotion. He is altogether too much like some bad dream and we would rather not be reminded of it.

As to the mystery of why he is still here, we shall have to be content to put him down as a left-over without knowing precisely how he managed to achieve that humble status. A long time ago he wandered into the desert pretty much what he is now and found that he could survive there, partly no doubt because his demands are modest and he can satisfy them without exposing himself very much. He eats insects which are plentiful and he can do without water as well as without food for long periods. Like the members of certain very old human families he has little to be proud of except the achievements of his remote ancestors, and if he were capable of pride he might, like them, grow prouder just in proportion as he comes to be more and more remote in time from them and their virtues. Like such people, he also makes us wonder what became of all the greatness which was once in his race. Did the scorpion use up all the daring of his tribe in his one great exploit all those millions of years ago? Did he squander it all at once like the wits at the Mermaid Tavern, each of whom seemed resolved to:

> *Put his whole wit in one jest*
> *And live a fool the rest of his dull life?*

•

It is a pleasant fancy but one had better not put it into words when there are any paleontologists about. We honor the scorpion for his early achievement but it has to be admitted that he doesn't seem to have done much to be proud of in recent years.

THE VOICE OF THE DESERT

SIX

the moth and the candle

THE MOTH WHO SINGES HIS WINGS HAS POINTED MANY A
moral but he does not "desire" the flame, not even in the
dim way that the first scorpion to leave the water may
have "desired" to succeed in his dangerous adventure.
The moth accomplishes no purpose of his own and none
appropriate to nature at large. He is merely the victim of
a situation which can seldom have arisen before man put
in his appearance long after moths and many other insects
had developed a tropism which was usually harmless during millions of years.

A moth's wings beat faster when light falls upon his eyes, and when it falls more strongly on one eye than on the other, the wings on one side beat faster than those on the other. Irresistibly his flight curves toward the source and if he reaches it, he dies—a victim of one of the mistakes which nature sometimes makes because even she cannot foresee every eventuality.

But in the case of a certain moth which lives in the desert and of a certain candle which grows there the situation is different.

Almost anywhere in the Southwest you will find as a conspicuous feature of the landscape one or another of the yuccas with their large bundle of stiff, sword-sharp leaves and, in early summer, an incredibly tall spire of innumerable creamy white blossoms held high on a great spike which shot up suddenly from the middle of the sword cluster. Pass by again in the fall and the spire will be bearing handsome pods which split open as they dry and scatter innumerable shiny black seeds on the sand. Though a bit difficult to gather, the pods make a fine addition to a winter bouquet and those who gather them often notice that each is perforated by at least one hole from which some insect has obviously emerged.

Sometimes the collector will search for a "perfect" specimen but perfect ones are not to be found. The "infestation" was necessary. Either the ovary from which the pod developed was "infested" or it didn't mature. Thereby hangs a tale as strange as any the desert has to tell and in certain important respects the most difficult to explain of all the strange tales which are told of the interdependence of insects and flowers. The hole was made by the larva of a moth, and just to make the question we are about to ask as neat as possible, it happens that certain species of yucca are still commonly called by the name which the Spaniards gave them: Our Lord's Candle.

Does Pronuba yuccasella, the moth in question, "desire" this particular candle? Please wait until you have heard the whole story before you answer.

Everybody—or at least everybody old enough to have been a child before directer methods of sex instruction came into fashion—knows about the bees and the flowers. If he did not lose all interest in the subject as he began to realize its remoter personal implications, he probably now knows at least in a very general way that many plants depend upon many insects and some, even, upon certain birds, to help them in what the eighteenth century liked to call "their nuptial rites." Orchard growers tend bees principally to increase their yield of apples and plums and pears; Darwin wrote a classic on the pollination of orchids; the Smyrna fig would not fruit in California until the particular wasp which acts as marriage broker for it in the Near East was imported to perform his function here, etc., etc.

But in every known case except that of the moth and the candle it is a somewhat one-sided affair with all the "intention" being on the part of the flower. Though the insect may be lured by a scent which it likes—even by the stench of rotten meat in the case of certain tropical blossoms pollinated by flesh-eating flies—and though he may be rewarded with nectar or with edible pollen, he does not do anything directly calculated to fertilize the flower. Sometimes the flower is so constructed that, for instance, the insect cannot get at the nectar without brushing against the pollen-bearing anthers and then against a stigma which will ultimately conduct the gene-bearing protoplasm of the pollen down to the ovules below. But he does not deliberately fertilize the plant and it would not affect his chances of passing on the torch to his posterity if the flower were not fertilized. The plant uses the insect but there is no active cooperation on the insect's part.

Consider, on the other hand, what happens in the unique case of the yucca and its attendant moth. In the first place, though there are many species of yuccas, only a single one of them—and it does not grow in this region—appears to be capable of getting along without the moth upon which all the rest depend. Moreover the moths, in their turn, are no less completely dependent upon the yuccas because their larva cannot feed upon anything except its maturing seeds. But this situation, which is odd without being unique, is not all. What *is* unique is the fact that the moth goes through a series of purposeful actions which have no other function except to fertilize a flower which could not be fertilized in any other way. If we naïvely interpreted its actions, we should find ourselves compelled to say that it "knows what it is doing."

The classic observation was made seventy-five years ago by the remarkable Missouri entomologist, Charles V. Riley, though the subject has been much studied and written about since Riley himself fully described the crucial, incredible event as he observed it on a cultivated species grown in the neighborhood of St. Louis. Several different insects frequent the flowers to eat the nectar or the pollen but perform no service in return. Meanwhile the female of the indispensable moth rests quietly in the half-closed blossoms.

When evening comes she goes in turn to several of the flowers just opening for their one night of perfect bloom. While the male, who has already done his duty, flutters uselessly about, she collects from the anthers a ball of the pollen which is surrounded by a sticky gum to prevent its accidental dispersal. After she has collected under her chin a mass somewhat larger than her head, she climbs the pistil of a different flower and into it she inserts her egg tube about a third of the way down from the top and injects several eggs. However she "knows" that if she left it at that her larva would have nothing to feed on. Accordingly, she mounts the rest of the way up the pistil, deposits the pollen ball on the stigma, and moves her head back and forth to rub the pollen well in. She eats neither nectar nor pollen. She gets no immediate benefit from her action. It has no purpose other than to fertilize the flower.

The insect which does these remarkable things is nothing much to look at—a little inch-long moth, silvery white in color and, so far as anyone knows, quite conventional in behavior except during the one great moment when it is impelled to act as though it knew a great deal about the physiology of plants as well as about the life history of its own species.

Most of what happens after the fertilization of the flower follows a familiar pattern. The flowers wither and a few days later the wormlike larva can be found. In time it will bore its way out of the maturing pod, drop to the ground, spin a cocoon a few inches below the surface, and there transform itself into an adult completely equipped to repeat, next year, the whole complicated process. Since there are commonly not more than two larvae per pod, they eat only a few of the perhaps two hundred seeds which the pod produces. From the standpoint of the yucca it is a very good arrangement since the sacrifice of a few seeds is a small price to pay for a very efficient job of fertilization. The staggering question for anyone who has committed himself to "explaining" nature is simply this: How on earth was such a system of mutual cooperation for individual ends ever worked out?

Evidently the yucca and the yucca moth came to their mutual understanding a long time ago—certainly before the plant genus had evolved the many species now flourishing—because, with the one exception previously mentioned, they all seem to be signatories to the agreement; certainly, also, long enough ago for the Pronuba moth to have itself evolved into at least several distinguishable species, because those which visit certain yuccas are slightly different from those which visit others. On the other hand, moth and yucca have not always worked together, because the flower continues to secrete a nectar which now merely attracts useless insects of various sorts and presumably it learned to do that at a time before Pronuba got into the habit of paying a visit on business of her own for which no honeyed inducement is necessary.

Apparently, sometime during the millennia when the two were engaged in a late phase of their evolution and separating themselves into the different species of moth and yucca, they must themselves have kept together. "Wherever thou goest I go," said the moth, because, again with the one single exception, where a yucca is native, so is a Pronuba. Attempt to grow the former outside its range and it may flower very nicely. But "no moth, no seed" seems to be the absolute rule.

William Trelease, student and monographer of the yucca
genus, calls attention to the fact that "the mutual dependence seems absolute" and he then permits himself a cautious, scientific understatement when he remarks that the
fact is "no doubt of the greatest suggestiveness," though
"its meaning has escaped both botanists and zoologists."

Now the relatively simple one-sided arrangement which
is so prevalent in the plant world is difficult enough to
understand. Geology seems to demonstrate that the earliest flowering plants depended, as the conifers do today,
upon the chance that some of their abundant pollen would
be carried by the wind to the waiting ovaries. Then, since
all organic matter is potentially edible by something, it is
assumed that certain insects got into the habit of eating
pollen, accidentally got some of it entangled in the hair on
their bodies as many still do, and accidentally rubbed some
of it off on the stigmas of the other flowers they visited.
Since, for the plant, this was more effective than wind pollination and involved less waste of vital material, those
plants which were most attractive to insects got along best.
And as the degree of attractiveness accidentally varied,
"natural selection" favored those which were most attractive, until gradually all the devices by which plants lure
insects or birds—bright colored petals, nectar which serves
the plant in no direct way, and perfume which leads the
insect to the blossom; even the "guide lines" which sometimes mark the route to the nectar glands—were mechanically and necessarily developed.

Gardeners usually hate "bugs," but if the evolutionists
are right, there never would have been any flowers if it
had not been for these same bugs. The flowers never waste

their sweetness on the desert air or, for that matter, on the jungle air. In fact, they waste it only when nobody except a human being is there to smell it. It is for the bugs and for a few birds, not for men, that they dye their petals or waft their scents. And it is lucky for us that we either happen to like or have become "conditioned" to liking the colors and the odors which most insects and some birds like also. What a calamity for us if insects had been color blind, as all mammals below the primates are! Or if, worse yet, we had had our present taste in smells while all the insects preferred, as a few of them do, that odor of rotten meat which certain flowers dependent upon them abundantly provide. Would we ever have been able to discover thoughts too deep for tears in a gray flower which exhaled a terrific stench? Or would we have learned by now to consider it exquisite?

The whole story, as it is usually told, of how flowers developed is thus a rather tall tale, as indeed the whole story of evolution is. But it does fall just short of the completely incredible even though we are likely to feel an additional strain when we begin to bring in the more remarkable features and find ourselves compelled to believe in the gradual blind development of the more intricate devices by which a flower is often adapted to some particular insect or bird and the exact correspondence between, say, the length of a given flower's tube and the length of the moth's proboscis or the hummingbird's bill which is going to reach down into it. But when we come to Pronuba and the yucca we get something more staggering still. That two different organisms should have simultaneously adapted themselves one to another is, if I understand the laws of probability, at least four times as improbable as that one should have adapted itself to the other. I am not saying I don't believe it did. On the whole I think I do, at least with one reservation. But sometimes I can't help saying to myself, "A man who will believe that will believe anything."

Since Darwin's day the fact that evolution did, somehow or other, take place has been made overwhelmingly clear. Because that fact could not really be doubted, most students felt compelled to accept what seemed to be the best available explanation of "how" it could possibly have happened. Yet the fact remains that a great many students have been just a little unhappy about that "how" and that a good deal of the work which has been done since Darwin's day has been concerned with an attempt to make the whole thing seem a little more credible.

Nearly everybody came to feel that Darwin's summary reliance on minute, accidental variation and natural selection was a bit too casual. The discovery that organisms were capable of sudden big-step "mutations" as well as minute variations helped. All sorts of experiments were designed to prove that some slight accidental advantage like the lighter color of a mouse living on sand really did increase significantly its chances of survival. The mathematically minded got into the game, notably Sir Ronald Aylmer Fisher who recently summarized in formidable equations his contention that chance is not chance when statistically studied and that the "progress" made in the course of evolution was no more merely fortuitous than the profits of the proprietor of a roulette wheel are. Given time enough he is bound to win. The "laws of probability" take the chanciness out of chance.

All of this helps. But one might as well admit also that the work done since Darwin constitutes a tacit admission on the part of the investigators that they would feel a bit more comfortable about the whole business if it could be made less hard to swallow, that quite possibly there is some factor operating which has not been taken proper account of. And when we come to the case of Pronuba and its elaborate working arrangement with the yucca we have an especially hard nut to crack. Accident, mutation, selection, statistical probability, etc., all seem to leave it a little mysterious still. Even granted a very long time for the thing to work itself out, we seem to be approaching the limits of credibility. It has been argued, to take the most extravagant case, that if a hundred apes were to bang away at a hundred typewriters for a long enough time, then, sooner or later, one of them would have to compose accidentally "Paradise Lost," complete and exact to the last comma. But do we believe that he ever would?

Many would admit that most of the difficulties could be made to vanish if only we might assume the intrusion of some factor not wholly accidental and mechanical. If there were only some intelligence, however feeble; some intention, however dim; some power of choice, however weak, which the evolving organism could have used to take advantage of the opportunities which chance provided. If only, in other words, the whole process of evolving life were not assumed to be so lifeless.

Nevertheless, most of the scientists who would even admit the convenience of such an assumption are aghast at the suggestion that it might be made. They throw up their hands in horror crying, "Teleology," "Vitalism," "Lamarckian nonsense," and the rest. There is no evidence, they say. And if you go beyond evidence you open the way to the most baseless speculations. The whole enterprise of science might just as well be given up. "No, no, no. Hard as it may be to swallow the official version of how either the Pronuba moth or Homo sapiens came to be what he is, you must not ask us to admit the possibility that there is purpose at work in the universe at large or even that the scorpion who came to land and the moth which joined up with the yucca had the dimmest conception of what he was doing."

We would be particularly happy, they say, to argue the whole question out in connection with your moth because, of all the highly evolved creatures, the insects are notoriously the most completely in the grip of their reflexes and their instinctive patterns of behavior. On the one hand, their life histories are extraordinarily complex. The spider's web, the wasp's wise provision of living but paralyzed prey for its young, and the complicated organization of ant society, are unparalleled in their intricate effectiveness by the procedures of any other creature except man. Entomology is one long tale of marvels. Yet, on the other hand, no other creatures are demonstrably so incapable of varying the set pattern of their behavior, so demonstrably unaware of what they are doing, or of why they do it. Thus the very class of animals which appears superficially to be the most purposeful is the very one in which not only purpose but even the possibility of consciousness seems most obviously absent. They are capable of behavior a thousand times more impressive than any a dog could ever rise to, yet a dog is far more intelligent. Not mentality of any kind but the reflexes established by chance are what produce the greatest wonders and those "evidences of design" which seem, at first sight, so convincing.

This makes a strong case against the simple assumption that purpose in the universe at large or intelligent planning in an individual animal species furnishes a sufficient explanation for what has happened in the course of evolution. Probably most of the mechanisms which science has so painstakingly explored really have operated effectively. But does this really demonstrate that something besides mechanism, say merely some very dim awareness and purpose, has never, to return to the word chosen a moment ago, "intervened" to tip the balance in one direction or another, to make the successful working out of some such arrangement as that of the moth with the yucca easier to understand than it is on the basis of a purely mechanical process? And are there not, after all, some observable phenomena which hint at powers present in even a modern insect which make such intervention not unthinkable?

We must grant that the insects as we know them today really do seem to come close to being those mere mechanisms which Descartes and the Cartesians insisted that all animals really are. Perhaps nobody—not even the most extreme mechanist—would today maintain, as Descartes did, that when a dog howls with pain he only *seems* to be suffering because he merely "operates like a watch by springs" and cannot feel anything; or that, as one of Descartes' disciples put it, all animals "eat without pleasure, they cry without pain, they grow without knowing it; they desire nothing, they fear nothing, they know nothing." But much of the time many insects really do seem to be almost purely mechanical.

Nevertheless, "much of the time" is not the same thing as "always." As a matter of fact, one single incontrovertible instance of an insect which did not behave mechanically, which exhibited desire, or will, or the power to choose a preferable alternative, would be enough to make it not only possible but probable that he had powers which might intervene in the course of evolution even now. Those powers would suggest that his primitive ancestors may have been able to intervene more effectively before they came—as they may have—to rely more and more on the instincts into which acquired habits gradually hardened. In man, "conditioned reflexes" are usually something which do not precede but succeed acts directed by consciousness. Why may not the conditioned reflexes of the insect have arisen in the same way out of habits of behavior first acquired with the help of his dim consciousness?

But can an "incontrovertible instance" of purposeful behavior in insects be cited? That would seem to be the crucial question and the answer to it is that quite a number of instances can be cited which are at least not usually controverted even though they are often brushed aside.

Take for example a few recently cited by Evelyn Cheesman, a recognized authority who was for many years Curator of Insects for the Zoological Society of London. Most of her most recent book, *Insects: Their Secret World*, is concerned with describing what appear to be the fixed, invariable, perhaps almost completely unconscious, behavior patterns of insects, including even the highest. But there is a last chapter called "Individual Actions" in which she cautiously describes observed cases where instinctive behavior seems to have been momentarily superseded by a purposeful action designed to meet an unusual situation.

I shall choose only one, partly because it is both simple and comic.

The individual which exhibited this instance of what must amount to genius in an insect was a solitary wasp of the New Hebrides. It had got into the habit of visiting Miss Cheesman's breakfast table for sweets and she had got into the habit of performing little experiments upon it. When it had retired to its tiny burrow for the day and stood just within the entrance on guard against intruders who might steal its larder of insect food, the experimenter would tap threateningly with a pair of forceps and the wasp would emerge to do battle, leaping upon the forceps and trying to bite into the steel.

". . . When the forceps remained still she seemed satisfied that the enemy was slain and would return to the burrow, rushing in head foremost as was her habit. Directly she turned her back to do this I would give her a little tap. Now what is interesting is that such habits are hereditary. That particular species always enters her burrow head first . . . but that particular wasp after several times having a tap from the forceps wouldn't turn her back again. She lowered herself very cautiously backwards into the burrow, keeping a bright look-out for this treacherous enemy which pretended to be dead and then came to life again when she was not looking. It is an interesting point, because it proves once more that some insects are not completely hide-bound by their instincts, but that individuals can change a hereditary habit on occasions."

Why should Miss Cheesman and I after her make such a fuss about so small an event? Simply because upon its interpretation some very important implications depend. If this particular wasp could change its behavior to meet intelligently a new situation, then it was not a machine "wound up like a watch." It was not merely something to which things happen. It was also capable of playing an active not merely a passive role in "adjusting to circumstances." And if Pronuba, admittedly now a creature far less bright than a wasp, has or ever did have any similar capacities, then her working agreement with the yucca need not have been wholly the result of chance. She may have taken advantage of a situation which presented itself and, however feebly, played her part as an individual in the course of evolution.

To admit that is to make a thousand times less incredible the fact that every spring thousands of moths perform the actions without which neither the yucca nor the moth could produce another generation. But that is not all. It relieves us from the necessity of assuming that the universe has been, at least up to the appearance of man, as will-less, as purposeless, as meaningless—one must almost say as dead—as the orthodox view tends to assume.

Some of the reasons why this commonly *is* assumed are sound enough, at least as far as they go, but some of them are merely the result of a human weakness which scientists share with the rest of mankind. Mechanisms are much easier to study than intelligence or purpose are. A great deal of progress has been made during the last hundred years in understanding them and the scientists are probably right in saying that such progress would not have been made if they had permitted their determination to discover these mechanisms to be weakened by too ready a willingness to say, when faced with a problem, merely "intelligence," "purpose," etc. If we may be permitted the military terms with which recent years have made us all too familiar, their procedure was *tactically* sound because it served the immediate purpose. But it may be proving to be *strategically* unfortunate because it has resulted in a dogged adherence to a "nothing but" hypothesis which some believe is already being exposed as untenable.

A merely human weakness accounts for the fact that many scientists, like many laymen, hold onto a hypothesis both because they are stubborn and because the hypothesis implies something which they *want* to believe; because, to put it more brutally, it confirms a prejudice. And it is an amusing fact that the wholly mechanistic theory of insect behavior can be made to serve the interests of either of two diametrically opposed prejudices.

On the one hand, it is commonly upheld by atheists so fanatical that they are afraid to admit the reality of purpose or intelligence or will lest the admission lead somehow to a belief in God. On the other hand, one of the most fanatical insisters upon the dogma that never, under any circumstances, does an insect contribute anything to the seeming "wisdom" of its behavior was that sincere and orthodox Roman Catholic, Henri Fabre.

Probably he had never heard of the yucca moth. At least I remember no mention of it in the ten volumes of his *Souvenirs Entomologiques*. But it would have delighted him as a notable addition to his imposing collection of the elaborately effective procedures followed by creatures without intelligence. Every one of them was, he insisted, proof of the existence of a God who, in his wisdom, had contrived the little living machines which unconsciously do precisely what they need to do if they are to live their often outrageous lives.

Face to face with such phenomena as the cruel shrewd-

ness or seeming shrewdness of many parasites, he spoke of
"le savant brigandage de la vie"—the expert criminality of
life. And he never faced the problem which seems to arise
when one places the responsibility for such a villainous
system of exploitation directly upon a personal God. But
he never wavered. The wonders of instinct confirmed his
Catholic theology as conclusively as they confirm the athe-
ism of many mechanists.

Somewhere along the line of this argument, the less
trusting of my readers may have wanted to raise doubts
not so much concerning the argument itself as concerning
the alleged facts upon which it is based. Does Pronuba
really do any of these things it is said to?

After all, entomologists are always coming up with
wonders about ants, bees and what not. Laymen seldom
see them with their own eyes and if by any chance they
take an hour off to look, they are more likely than not to
see nothing remarkable. Insects take their time. For long
periods they behave in what seems like a completely wit-
less fashion—as Mark Twain discovered when he convinced himself that the ant and his extraordinary reputation for sagacity was a complete fraud.

The Mr. Riley who first told the world about Pronuba
was a distinguished entomologist. He had the confidence
of his professional brethren and textbook after textbook
has repeated his tale. But is it just possible that he was
overenthusiastic? How many other people have watched
the performance and can vouch for it from their own experience?

Well, I confess that the shadow of such doubts crossed
my own mind. Of the various references to Pronuba with

which I was familiar, only one after Riley's own seemed on internal evidence to be indubitably first hand. The most learned entomologist of this region where yucca flourishes confessed that he had never seen the performance and didn't know anybody who had. Not too willingly—since I knew the difficulties, which include, besides the dilatoriness of the insect, darkness, a limited blooming season, and flowers lifted high above one's head—I decided to try to see for myself. And not to sustain any suspense which any reader may feel, I did. Three times Pronuba demonstrated before my eyes how she performed the crucial act, mounting the pistil of the recently opened flower and with prolonged purposefulness rubbing the pistil vigorously to get the pollen well in.

Partly to avoid the possibility that some amateur alienist might telephone a mental hospital that for several evenings a maniac had been seen standing for two hours and more peering at yucca flowers with a flashlight, I decided to make my observations well out into the desert and some twenty miles from town. And for poetic if not for strictly scientific reasons it was a good idea. It is one thing to read about what Pronuba does. It would be quite another to see her at work in a neighbor's back yard. But the performance belongs properly among the mysteries which one can only appreciate fully when the context is remote from the human and as exclusively as possible in that of almost timeless nature.

The moonless night was brilliant with stars. In the distance a coyote pack obligingly set up its chorus which is as wild a sound as one is likely to hear anywhere. And then, presently, there was Pronuba, even more insignificant looking than I had expected her to be, performing her delicate operation precisely, no doubt, as her ancestors had performed it millions of times during millions of springs. On the horizon the lights of town were just visible. In all that town few knew about, perhaps none had ever seen, the strange actions of this silent moth without whom the tall spires of flowers would never conceive their seeds and without whom, therefore, the whole race of yuccas would gradually die out. It was for the almost invisible moth, not for you or me or any aesthetically appreciative human spectator, that the great masses of flowers were lifted high.

As little Pronuba moved her head back and forth I remembered the question once asked by the American essayist Charles D. Stewart after he had described what looked like a remarkably purposeful action on the part of a spider who suddenly cut the main cable of his web and thereby sent flying an intruder of another species with designs upon an insect caught in the owner's web. "Is it God who is doing these things," Stewart asked, "or is it a spider?"

Fabre would have answered without hesitation, "God." Most biologists would reply with equal assurance, "Neither." But few are willing to admit what seems to me not wholly improbable—namely that the spider himself had something to do with it.

the mouse that never drinks

FOR SEVERAL YEARS I WAS ON QUITE INTIMATE TERMS WITH
the common house mouse and I attempted to celebrate his
charm in print. There is, therefore, nothing odd in the fact
that I have recently been associating with the so-called
kangaroo rat of the desert, who is, really, more mouselike
than ratlike. I keep a pair of them in a glass case from
which they enjoy frequent sorties to sit on the palm of my
hand, rest in my pocket, or run through paper tubes which
they seem to accept as easily recognizable substitutes for
an underground passageway.

So far as I am concerned there is, I say, nothing odd about this. But there is something very odd indeed about my companions. In fact the kangaroo rat is famous as "the mouse that never drinks," and because of his incredible abstention from all potations, he has attracted the attention—considerably more unwelcome than mine—of laboratory scientists who have analyzed his blood, examined his urine, and imposed fantastically abnormal conditions upon him to force him to break his inveterate teetotalism.

They find that it can be done. But it is not certain that in nature he ever does so. Obviously he is the most triumphant imaginable example of adaptation to the most characteristic desert difficulty, the absence of water. It is no wonder that the largest of all the kangaroo rats lives in Death Valley, the hottest and driest spot in the United States, where it sometimes never rains at all for a year and more. To get along without is the most radical solution in any economy of scarcity.

In the appearance of the sleek little creatures there is nothing to suggest the underprivileged. Their manner is exuberant and, unlike many desert plants, they do not look at all desiccated—which as a matter of fact they are not. You would never suspect that they did not drink like any other flourishing animal. In fact it is hard to believe that they don't. And to realize fully just how extraordinary that fact is one should know them personally as well as technically. But let us begin with technicalities.

From the zoologist's standpoint the kangaroo rat is actually neither a rat nor a mouse because he belongs to a different order of the rodent family, one of the reasons being that he has twenty teeth while both Rattus and Mus have to get along with only sixteen. Still, his general appearance is mouselike enough. He has thick, silky brown hair and a pointed bewhiskered nose. His crowning glory —worn at the opposite end from that on which crowning glories are usually worn—is a handsome tail half again as long as all the rest of his body and with a furry banner at the end, much like that on the tail of a lion. Moreover, this tail turns out to be very useful as well as ornamental.

Actually there are some sixteen different species of kangaroo rats resident in the arid parts of the West and one of them, also found about Tucson, goes in for a fine decorative touch by choosing to have his banner a contrasting white. Mine, whose scientific name is Dipodomys merriami, is the smallest of the tribe and consists of about four inches of body with six or more of tail. I choose him rather than his larger cousin because he happens to be the one whose independence of any external water supply has been tested and vouched for by relentless laboratory experimenters.

Dipo's large black eyes are a clear enough indication that his habit is nocturnal, and the casual traveler ordinarily sees him only as some sort of small rodent hurrying across the road in the headlights of an automobile. In nature he makes extensive burrows entered through many surface holes and usually under a considerable mound of earth, perhaps fifteen feet in circumference and often so thoroughly tunneled just below the surface that it will collapse if one attempts to walk across it.

Other desert rodents, ground squirrels and gophers, make similar holes, but the Dipo's residence is usually recognizable by the fact that the mound is elevated well above the surrounding surface of the ground. Apparently, however, he does not always have this well-constructed home to himself. It seems that rabbits sometimes enlarge one of his entrances and move in. So probably does an occasional snake, who cannot be a very welcome house guest. Moreover, though Dipos probably have a home base, they take refuge in the nearest hole when danger threatens and they must often be surprised by what they find there.

In Australia there is also a kangaroo rat which really is a kangaroo—a marsupial that is, complete with a pouch in which to carry its young. Sticklers say it should be called rather a "rat-kangaroo" just as, so these same sticklers insist, an aviator ought to be called a "manbird" and only an ornithologist a "birdman." But, in any event, Dipo is a rodent, not a marsupial, and the only true American marsupial, the 'possum, does not live in the arid Southwest. Nevertheless Dipo gets his common name from the obvious fact that he *looks* like a kangaroo—because of his long tail, his stubby little forelimbs which are not much good for walking, and his habit of sitting or jumping on his long hind legs. Like a real kangaroo he will also box with a neighbor while sitting on his tail and striking out with his hands.

In the gobbledygook of technical description, all the species of Dipodomys are said to be "admirably adapted to a bipedal, saltatory existence." In other words, they jump on their hind legs! Even in captivity and though normally rather placid creatures, they may, when some not-too-amiable brush between one and another takes place, suddenly begin to bound erratically a foot and a half high and to land after each bound no one can predict where. But why? The ability to do without water is obviously a very useful accomplishment for a desert dweller. What good are a disproportionately long tail and the ability to make prodigious, unpredictably erratic leaps?

There must be some reason, because in other faraway deserts, those in Africa for instance, other creatures have adapted themselves to the same "bipedal, saltatory existence." The African jumpers and the American are not descended from a common ancestor who just happened to develop this habit. The African jerboa, even though he looks and acts like a kangaroo rat and is also a rodent, is not even very closely related. His analogue of the Australian desert is also not descended from either of the other two long tailed, short fore-legged desert creatures. Plainly we are again faced with a case of "convergence" like that of the desert cacti of America and the desert Euphorbias of Africa. Two different animals and two different plants have independently developed useful tricks for living in arid country. And the tricks are so similar that the two organisms have come to look very much alike. But the utility of the devices is evident in the case of the plants, not nearly so evident in that of the animals. Still, though no one is quite sure what the answer to the riddle is, a guess seems pretty probable.

Dipo can walk, or rather hobble, when he wants to. When he is tranquil that is usually what he does. But when he becomes excited or afraid, he begins to bound, switching his tail in the air as he leaps. And it is the switch of the long tail which makes his course unpredictable. Whether or not he himself knows where he is going to land is a question; certainly nobody else does. And that must be a great help when being pursued by a predator, especially an owl or a hawk. When one of them swoops at a Dipo, the Dipo usually turns out to be somewhere else.

That must have saved many a life in Africa and Australia as well as in America. And if you accept the most mechanical theory of evolution, then the more erratically a rodent leaped and the longer tail he had, the better were his chances to survive and to hand on his longer tail to a goodly number of progeny.

Other kinds of rodents didn't develop in the same direction because most of them live where cover is available. But in the desert cover is scarce and the ability to elude capture by unpredictable movement much more important. On this assumption the tuft at the end of the tail, which is as characteristic of the jerboa as it is of the kangaroo rat, simply makes the tail more effective as a rudder. One observer reports that a captive Dipo who had lost a considerable part of his tail in some accident, still leaped high but landed any old way instead of on his feet.

Among themselves Dipos seem rather quarrelsome. Mine, the merriami, are said to be the most peaceable of the tribe, and it is also said that for that reason several individuals of this species can be kept together in captivity. I have not found it so. My pair, even though they are male and female, have to be kept separated most of the time or they will soon take to boxing and from boxing to biting in a manner alarming to anyone anxious to keep them in good health. They seem, on the other hand, to have little fear of man and no tendency, even under provocation, to be aggressive toward him. They will run away if you approach them at liberty, but once caught, they will rest quietly on a human hand and, in fact, often come to it if one reaches down into a cage. It is said that even when roughly handled, merriami, at least, will make no attempt to bite, and mine have showed no resentment even when, on occasion, I have had to end a fight quickly by lifting one suddenly by the tail. Obviously they are very satisfactory pets, requiring a minimum of care. With a hopper of seeds there is no reason, so far as I can see, why they might not be left unattended for weeks. At least there is no water problem to be met. Mine have had none during the three months I have had them. And that brings us to Dipo's most extraordinary claim to fame.

How absolute is the independence of water? How is the seemingly impossible accomplished? The closer these questions are pushed, the more surprising the answers are.

To begin with, one should realize that many desert animals, like many desert plants, can get along on far less water than would suffice for the survival of most creatures. Sometimes it is said that even the jack rabbit does not drink, though this is so far from being absolutely true that I have often seen him taking a long draught from my birdbath. Quite possibly he can get along for a long time without any water, possibly he can get along indefinitely, but he drinks gladly and deep when he gets a chance. What is more important, the jack rabbit eats succulent green food when he can get it and is a great depredator of flower gardens when he gets a chance at them. With him it is not a question of doing without water but simply of getting the comparatively little which is indispensable from his food instead of in liquid form.

The same is true in the case of many desert creatures. The road runner also visits the birdbath, but since he eats such other animals as snakes, lizards and mice which have a good deal of water in their blood, he is in much the same position as the rabbit who likes a tender watery morsel when he can get it. The pack rat, another desert dweller, can, it has been demonstrated, get along without drinking at all. But he also must have succulent food. Dipo, on the other hand, belongs in an entirely different class. It is not only that he can get along without water. He will not take it if it is offered to him. And he does not have to have any succulent food either. *He can live indefinitely on the driest of dry seeds.*

This fact has been abundantly demonstrated by brutally thorough and rigorously controlled experiments. Kept under desert conditions of heat and of dryness for fifty-two days and fed on an exclusive diet of dried barley seeds, Dipodomys merriami not only lived but, when subjected to a post-mortem examination, showed no diminution in the proportion of water to total body weight; and that remained true even of those of the victims who gained in total weight during the course of the experiment. "Control" individuals who were given access to watermelon during the same period and who ate some of it retained no more water in their blood or tissues than did those who had eaten only dry food. As a matter of fact, Dipodomys needs to maintain the same water content in his blood as other rodents and will die from dehydration at about the same degree of deficiency in this respect.

The secret, then, is not merely the one we have met so often—rigid economy in the expenditure of water. In the first place, you cannot save what you have not been able to get. In the second place, Dipodomys isn't even as stingy in this respect as some other creatures. Unlike some insects and all birds, he does not save water by voiding uric acid only in solid form, though his urine is about twice as concentrated as that of the white rat, and when fed on dry food his excrement is forty-five percent water as compared with sixty-five percent for the white rat. He does save in another way because, unlike most mammals, he uses no water for heat regulation either by sweating from the pores of the skin or from the mouth by panting. As pitiless experimenters have demonstrated, only when subjected to heat of a nearly fatal degree will he slobber slightly at the mouth, thus using a little of the precious water to try to save himself in extremity. And one reason for his nocturnal habit probably is that he can keep relatively cool in his burrow during the day, thus avoiding the risk of being called upon to pant.

But no economy can explain a complete getting along without. Dipo's secret is simply—if you can call it simple —that he *manufactures* his own water from the dry materials present in starchy foods. In one sense the chemistry is elementary enough. Starch is a hydrocarbon and therefore contains hydrogen. Oxygen is abundant in the air he breathes. And as every high school student of chemistry knows, water is H_2O—or a chemical combination of one part oxygen with two parts hydrogen. You can make it by one of the simplest of laboratory experiments if you explode a mixture of the two. But you can't do it effectively enough in your own body, as Dipo does, who takes it all in a day's work. The result is what the biochemists call "the water of metabolism" and for Dipo, with his very unusual metabolism, it is no doubt a routine matter. The only way you can force him to drink is to feed him on a diet so largely protein that he does not get enough hydrocarbon to furnish him with hydrogen. In that unhappy state he will drink water—I wonder if it tastes very nasty—when it is given him.

If in one sense this is all simple enough, in another it

is as mysterious as anything very well could be. Dipo "evolved" the capacity to produce water of metabolism sufficiently to supply his needs and they are quite as great as those of many other desert creatures. It is obviously a gift with great "survival value." But why didn't all the creatures, some of which certainly sometimes perish of thirst, "evolve" it too? What inborn capacity, if that is what it was, made him potentially independent of an external water supply?

Moreover, while Dipodomys was evolving his unusually effective gift for manufacturing water internally, he had also to evolve at the same time a certain special efficiency in an organ which is part of the standard equipment of all except the very simplest animals, and actually has at least an analogue even in the one-celled protozoa: namely the kidney. One authority on this organ, Dr. Homer W. Smith, Professor of Physiology at the New York University College of Medicine, enthusiastically maintains that the whole story of evolution can be told in terms of the evolution of the kidney. He has also the highest admiration for Dipo's renal equipment.

Most of us, it seems, do the kidney, whether our own or that of other animals, less than justice. We think of it as merely an organ of excretion, but it is actually far more than that. It is responsible for that "internal environment" in which all our vital organs and the very cells themselves live, isolated from the air which would be fatal. Ever since the days of the first vertebrates it has had a very difficult job to accomplish. So far as the invertebrate animals which still live in the sea are concerned, they have the same salt content as that of the sea itself, and all their rudimentary kidneys have to do is to get rid of any excess solids, including salt. But all vertebrates, including of course all those which live on land, have to maintain in their bodies blood of a density which must not vary except within small limits and which, as it happens, is considerably less dense than that of sea water.

There are those who believe that its density corresponds to that of the once less salty sea at the time when the first vertebrates developed. But however that may be, the kidneys have to see to it that the density remains constant by eliminating excess water or excess minerals as the case may be. To get rid of excess salts they must deliver to the bladder for excretion a fluid much denser than the blood. But there is a limit to what they can do in preparing this concentrated fluid. Men and nearly all animals will quickly die if they drink a quantity of sea water, because it is far denser than any fluid their kidneys can concentrate and it simply increases that oversaltiness of the blood of which thirst is a sign. So far as is known, only one animal can drink sea water, for though sea birds have sometimes been assumed capable of it, they probably are not. The one animal who can—as the reader has probably guessed—is our hero Dipodomys.

He does not want to waste water merely to get rid, as he must, of excess mineral matter. Hence he has developed an unparalleled capacity to concentrate urine. Man cannot concentrate a fluid to more than 4.2 times the osmotic concentration of his blood plasma, but the kangaroo rat is capable of concentrating to 17 times the density of his blood and that is considerably denser than sea water. Hence if he is forced by a special diet to drink when only sea water is available, he can quench his thirst with that.

You and I may be amazed at this feat without being greatly stirred by it. But to a man with Dr. Smith's enthusiasm for the kidney it implies a feat worthy of the highest admiration, and with real fervor he lets himself go with a flat statement: "The kidney of the kangaroo rat can concentrate to the greatest extent of any known animal."

Feeling that I have, perhaps, not admired Dipo sufficiently for this particular talent, I let him stand for a few minutes in the palm of my hand. I see again that he is an unusually attractive little beast but that there is nothing in his external appearance to reveal what a physiological marvel he is. Nor does he himself seem to be aware of it. Like any ordinary mouse he seems a very modest little creature. Why should the heart of mortal man, or the kidney of mortal mouse, be proud? God, the blind chance which is responsible for all evolution, or, perhaps, something somehow in between, has given him the kidneys he needs to live comfortably in the desert. Whether man and mouse want much or little here below depends on how you look at it. But both sometimes get what they want.

Some chapters ago we commented on the fact that there are three ways of meeting the water problem—by economizing, by storing, and by lying low. Dipo introduces us to the fourth and most radical method: making your own. Certain other animals probably make some, but so far as is known, the kangaroo rat is the only one who can make enough to be entirely independent.

Making your own is not only the most radical solution; it is also the only one of the four which is not adopted to a greater or lesser degree by both plants and animals. In other words, no plant can exist, as Dipo can, without some external source of water. In the damp air of the tropics many plants grow upon trees, have no roots in the ground, and depend upon rainfall or dew. But no plant in the desert can do that because rainfall is too infrequent and dew nonexistent, except perhaps in winter. In air so dry, the dew point is usually at a below-freezing temperature —which is certainly not to be looked for except during the early mornings of midwinter. And no plant of either the desert or the tropics can imitate Dipo's feat. Plants do not eat hydrocarbons from which the kangaroo rats make their water. As a matter of fact plants make hydrocarbon and to do that you have to use up water, not create it.

Moreover, though all of the three less radical solutions have been hit upon by both plants and animals, they do not seem to be equally characteristic of both. On the whole, plants tend to store as well as to economize; on the whole, animals tend to have little or no provision for storing. They can get along on little and hence go long periods without replenishing the supply, but that is principally because they use so little, not because they put aside a supply to be drawn upon. Dipo doesn't. Even his blood is not unusually watery at any time.

There is, however, at least one desert animal who may violate the general rule and is worth mentioning for that reason, as well as for some others. He is the desert tortoise, a great lumbering fellow, scaly skinned and hard backed, who may be almost a foot in length, eight inches wide, and stand five inches off the ground. He is a formidable looking creature who appears, as most turtles do, not only very ancient as a type but almost equally ancient as an individual. He also looks rather threatening, though he is actually completely inoffensive—which all turtles certainly are not, as anyone who has ever had any experience with a snapper well knows. Though quite frequently found in very dry, cactus-covered desert areas, he is always a surprise when one comes across him crawling slowly along or holed up headfirst in some little recess under a rock.

It is also surprising to discover that, despite his robustious appearance, he is a vegetarian who favors salads of one sort or another and in captivity eats lettuce with as much enthusiasm as turtles show for anything. He sleeps in the shade at midday and he sleeps through most of the winter. Moreover he seems to have been born old as well as resigned and wise. If you should happen across one, you will see that he is a kind of box-turtle, though the front of his under shell is not hinged and he cannot shut himself in completely. You may be puzzled by a curious triangular projection in front and wonder what he uses it for. He uses it to fight with when a tank battle between two individuals takes place.

This turtle, of course, gets his water from the succulent vegetables he eats. But the most remarkable thing about him is the way in which he stores it up against a rainless day. Just under his upper shell is an unusually large bladder which in good times is full of water to be drawn upon as needed. Obviously he could be called the camel of our deserts. As a matter of fact, I shouldn't be at all surprised if he could far outdo the real camel's somewhat over-publicized ability to go for a long time without a drink.

Among animals, then, Dipo and the desert tortoise represent two ultimates in adaptation. What plant, I have been wondering, should get first prize in this same category? Some might say "the barrel cactus" which, even under conditions of extreme aridity, may hold in its pulpy center enough water to save a human life. But water storage to a greater or less degree is common among the cacti and my candidate is one which stores little water and yet represents a sort of ultimate in the twin arts of economy and lying low.

Wander down into the driest desert region in northern Sonora, Mexico, and you are likely to find lying about under thorny bushes certain amorphous masses of grayish wood eight inches or more in diameter. They look rather like a gnarled bur from some old apple tree; they have neither roots nor stems, and they seem about as dead as anything could be. Pick one up and you will find it heavy as well as dry, and quite hard—as little like a living plant as anything you can imagine.

This, however, is the resting stage of Ibervillea sonorae, a member of the gourd family. Sometime towards the end of May, it comes to life by sending out a few shoots upward and a few roots downward. It "knows" that Sonora's one season of scanty rainfall is about due and that it must be prepared to take advantage of it. If the rain does come, flowers and fruits appear before the whole thing dries up again into a state of suspended animation which seems almost as complete as that of a seed. At best, Ibervillea is not much to look at: a few straggling stems, small yellow flowers and, finally, a small berry-like fruit rather like a small, soft gourd. Moreover, membership in the gourd family is revealed by the structure of the flowers which, as in most gourds and melons, are "monoecious," i.e., separately sexed as male and female though both sorts are borne on the same plant.

Some years ago a specimen of Ibervillea was placed on exhibition in a glass case at the New York Botanical

Garden. There was no intention to have it grow, but it showed what it is capable of. For seven years, without soil or water, simply lying in the case, it put forth a few anticipatory shoots and then, when no rainy season arrived, dried up again, hoping for better luck next year.

My specimen, transplanted to a situation somewhat like its native one, has put forth its stems at the appropriate time. Just how much it could endure I do not know. I would be less reluctant to find out than I would be to feed my Dipos an abnormal diet, deprive them of water and bake them with heat until they frothed at the mouth, and then note whether those given sea water would survive while those which were denied even that died. But I would be reluctant to push to its limits even a vegetable. It is enough for me to know without experimentation that the vegetable psyche—if there is any such thing—is even more patient, persistent and enduring than the animal.

EIGHT

settlers—old and new

IT IS SOMETIMES SAID THAT IN SOUTHERN ARIZONA THE DOGS have no fleas. This is certainly an exaggeration though they do seem to have very few. Odd, you may say, because fleas are supposed to require nothing for their happiness except the dog himself. Yet here is a creature who has never really learned how to live well in the desert. Perhaps the dryness of the air is too much for him.

On the other hand, the law of compensation works for dogs too, and they are subject to a local annoyance. During the summer months all those near Tucson spend half their time running about on three legs—which many of them do not seem to mind too much until one of the remaining three is put out of commission. When that happens they have to do something about it and what the wiser of them do is to approach their masters with an uplifted paw from which the master then extracts a section of a little three- or four-seeded fruit provided with sharp projecting spines perhaps an eighth of an inch long. The seeds were only thumbing a ride into new territory and if fortune favors the seeds rather than the dogs, they will come up next summer as an inoffensive-looking prostrate weed with small compound leaves and humbly pretty little yellow flowers. Few inhabitants of the region have escaped some acquaintance with the fruit because it sometimes gets inside a human shoe and is said in the old days to have sometimes punctured a bicycle tire—whence the local name, "puncture vine," for the plant.

Many probably do not connect the fruit with the familiar weed, but Linnaeus knew all about it two hundred years ago and gave it its current botanical name—Tribulus terrestris. The first half of this name is Latin for those wicked iron balls with spikes so arranged that one is always pointing upwards. Medieval ingenuity scattered them over the ground when enemy cavalry was expected to attack. Linnaeus was only borrowing an ancient name for a thorny plant and I am not sure whether it was first applied to the seed or to the weapon. In any event, here is another case where nature was the first inventor of a device man later hit upon for himself.

But how did it happen that Linnaeus knew about this inconspicuous weed growing way out in Arizona at a time when even the Spanish fathers were but precariously established there? The answer to that question is simply that he didn't. As a matter of fact, Tribulus probably wasn't even there then. Today it seems at least as much at home as we do but, like us, it is really a native of the Old World and it came as an unnoticed colonist. Nobody is sure just when it arrived, but it was first noticed near the Pacific Coast in comparatively recent times and the pilgrim fathers of its tribe probably landed there. By now it is common as far east as Nebraska or Kansas and is found sometimes in the Atlantic states.

Thus, of plants as of people it is perfectly proper to ask, "Where did your forefathers come from?" The recent plant invaders have not, to be sure, ousted the natives as effectively as the white man has ousted the Indian, but if one goes back far enough it is often difficult to know who really is an aborigine. The Indians came from somewhere else and so, probably, did the cactus even if it got here a long time before they did.

Over the whole of the United States many of the most taken-for-granted plants were not here a few centuries ago, though they are now so thoroughly at home that sometimes only recorded history can distinguish the newcomers from those who have been here for thousands of years. The daisy and the Queen Anne's lace, so familiar in New England, are Europeans; so are the dandelion and the mullens of the East, the West, and everywhere else. Probably the Pilgrims had dandelions almost as soon as they had meadows, but there were none here before European man arrived.

Within our continent itself hardy pioneers, plant or even animal, go both west and east. Within the last quarter of a century the starling, so overly familiar in eastern cities, has been gradually advancing westward toward the Pacific Coast. Plants also have been moving in both directions for a long time. Few easterners who gather black-eyed susans know that they moved (or more probably were carried unintentionally as seed) from our own West within the period of our national history. Few who plant the giant "Russian" sunflower know that it belongs to an exclusively American genus which was taken to Russia in the nineteenth century, taught gigantism there, and then returned to us with the benefits of a foreign education. Probably the comrades who munch its seeds would deny its origin at the same time that they claimed credit for its improvement.

In Arizona alone there are some two hundred different plants which are recognized as having been introduced by man—in most cases unintentionally. Some of them arrived as the now dominant population did—westward across the continent from the eastern seaboard. But quite a few others came overland from the Pacific Coast or up from Mexico. And a number of those which moved in from the West are, like the Indian, Asiatic, not European, immigrants.

Meanwhile, perhaps an equal number of plants have been deliberately introduced or gone as stowaways from the New World to the Old. Everybody knows about tobacco, potatoes and Indian corn, but that is merely because they happen to be of great economic importance. Many European weeds came from the Americas and so, of course, do many now familiar European garden flowers, a surprising number of which are horticulturists' developments from California species.

Moreover, there are a few spectacular cases which it would astonish most Europeans to hear about. Most of the stately palm trees which grow along the Riviera (and for that matter in Hawaii) grow as natives only in California and a few places in Arizona. Or consider the so-called mimosa which seems so characteristic of southern France in the region around Grasse where it makes a very important contribution to the perfume industry. What could be more "typically French?" Actually it is a native of Mexico, Texas and Arizona, not of Europe at all. Sometime early in the seventeenth century it was imported into the famous gardens of the Cardinal Odorardo Farnese, a relative by marriage to the Borgias and the Médicis. It is quite possible that all the French "mimosas" came from that Italian garden and the botanical name of the plant, Acacia farnesiana, honors one of the more innocent activities of the Cardinal.

Botanists try to distinguish among plants introduced by human agency by calling those which grew only when man tends them, "cultivated"; those which linger more or less precariously after cultivation, "escaped"; and those which now go it completely alone, "adventitious." But it is sometimes impossible to distinguish sharply between the last two because there are some which are certainly almost, though not quite, capable of going it alone.

Perhaps the most familiar eastern example is the orange day lily which not only lingers but spreads for generations about the site of an abandoned house; perhaps the most conspicuous desert example is the straggling shrub with gaudy yellow and red blossoms, commonly called bird of paradise, which came up from South America into Mexico and is now so common in thickly inhabited portions of southern Arizona that one hardly knows whether to call it cultivated, escaped, or adventitious. In any event, a slow-motion movie of the United States since the sixteenth century would show the vegetative as well as the human population ebbing and flowing—mostly flowing—in all directions.

Nearly everywhere he goes man intentionally carries with him such directly useful plants and animals as can be persuaded to grow in whatever new country he is colonizing: cattle, sheep, horses, Indian corn, cotton, etc., etc. Sometimes he unknowingly brings animals which had once lived there but subsequently became extinct, as he did when he brought the horse to America. To the southwestern deserts he brought even the camel, which is said to have survived there as an escapee for forty years or more. The organisms which go along with him as stowaways are far more numerous. Wherever one of his ships lands, rats are pretty sure to go ashore with him. The dandelion follows him into almost every temperate climate, the cockroach into the tropics and the arctic as well.

Even today he is far less master of his environment than he likes to imagine. New destructive pests and new diseases make the headlines. No one notices the arrival of other organisms, desirable, undesirable or merely harmless. But they do not ask our permission to come. It is said that most of the earthworms of the northeastern part of the United States were killed during the Ice Age and that most of those now performing their indispensable service to agriculture in New England are of various European species unwittingly introduced by early colonists in the soil about the roots of imported plants. To find native American worms dominant you must go south of the Mason and Dixon Line. During the century just past, the winkle, beloved of cockneys, has invaded the Atlantic Coast.

Since the true desert areas constitute a very special and difficult environment, they are not readily colonized and in Arizona few if any plants except those under cultivation were intentionally introduced by man. Every conspicuous feature of the desert landscape has been there for a long, long time slowly adapting itself to heat and aridity, either here or in some other not too distant desert from which it could spread without the necessity of passing through any region unsuited to it. The vast majority of the nearly two hundred introduced plants counted in the flora of the state grow principally either in the portions not naturally desert, or in the neighborhood of houses or cultivated fields where conditions have been mitigated.

There is, however, one interesting exception which happens to be of some economic importance and is found everywhere on plains and mesas if not in full desert. Cattlemen have a popular name for it and call it "filaree," a word corrupted from the Spanish, and they are well aware of the plant because it is green in midwinter and is eaten by their herds when little else is available. I have found it blooming in January about my house in places where enough water is spilled to make the difference between natural desert and the slightly moister conditions of the mesas. It is believed to have been accidentally introduced at a very early time by the Spanish settlers, but it is really a European member of the wild geranium family.

The question how and when species were unintentionally introduced is quite as interesting as the question where they came from. In many cases the "when" can be answered only in such general terms as "long ago" or "recently," but the "how" is often pretty obvious. A few come with the seeds of useful and ornamental plants or in the soil around roots when the desired sorts are imported. A great many were certainly what botanists call "ballast weeds," delivered unintentionally to our shores by ships which dumped here the ballast loaded at some foreign port. Many western ones came mixed with the hay brought by early explorers and colonists. In fact it has been picturesquely suggested (though it can hardly be proved) that some already well-established inland when first observed may have been distributed along the way by Coronado and his horsemen when they made their long trek from Mexico into Kansas in the midsixteenth century, a good fifty years before any colony was established on the eastern seaboard.

The finding of Asiatic, not European, weeds in parts of Arizona and the Great Basin region would be a puzzle indeed, if it were not known that at one time alfalfa seed in considerable quantity was imported by the inhabitants of those regions from Siberia and Turkistan. And as is usual in such cases, more was imported than the importers knew. No sight is more characteristic of the wide-open West than the tumbleweeds which go bowling across the landscape in late summer or autumn and sometimes pile high along the fences. They are not all of one species, but one of the commonest in irrigated regions is the so-called Russian thistle which is actually a Eurasian and must have been recognized by the Indians as an importation because its Hopi name means "white man's plant."

It is an odd fact that the most completely cosmopolitan

of all plants and animals are the microscopic one-celled ones, just possibly because they are supposedly the oldest and have had the most time in which to colonize everywhere. Except for those which are parasitic on some special animal, nearly all the protozoa of fresh water are found everywhere in the world except in those parts eternally frozen. Before that fact was known biological specialists used to go exploring like the specialists in other fields in the hope of discovering new species. In the eighteen nineties, for instance, a distinguished Swiss protozoologist came all the way to the American Far West for that purpose. At first he considered his expedition not entirely a failure because he thought that he had found just one. But when he got back to Switzerland he found it there also.

To the curious who poke about as I often do in the out-of-the-way places so abundant in this region where so many places are still really out-of-the-way, nothing is more usual than the abandoned shack, the forgotten shaft of some one-man mine, or even a rather imposing collection of buildings with pieces of machinery rusting on a hillside where they were left perhaps half a century ago. They remind us that settlers do not always settle, that populations move away from as well as into sparsely occupied regions. And the same thing is true of nonhuman creatures, vegetable as well as animal. Throughout the West there are ghost towns and towns in the process of becoming ghosts as well as thriving new settlements. And there are plant communities precisely analagous to both. When such communities appear to have shrunk until they now occupy only small isolated areas, the botanists call them "relict floras." What has been happening to them is what happened to such a human community as Tombstone which once flourished, but now survives at all largely because tourist curiosity keeps it alive much as it keeps alive the bison herds and the flocks of wild turkeys now "protected" because people like to see them.

Such relict floras occur in many parts of the world, but they are especially conspicuous and perhaps especially common in regions like this where only a small margin makes life possible, and where organisms which have achieved very special adaptations to very special conditions cannot survive even slight changes. It is just possible that even the giant saguaro which grows nowhere else in the world except within a rather small area may be such a relict flora in an early stage of its coming extinction. I know of no evidence that it once grew much more widely, but it is certainly not reproducing itself at a rate which will maintain its dominance in many of the areas which it now does dominate. And in any event there are other plants which are obviously only lingering in one or more spots isolated by many miles from the only other communities of their kind. In many cases it is, for a change, not man but nature herself who is gradually making it impossible for them to live where they once flourished. Slight changes in temperature, or rainfall, or what-not are proving to be decisive, and we can only guess whether such minor changes in the flora really are only minor or whether they mark the beginnings of a change which, in the course of centuries or millennia, may change the whole face of the country as that of America or Europe has changed repeatedly during the course of the ages.

One case happens to interest me especially. In northern

Mexico there is a rather common tree with a white exfoliating bark rather like that of a sycamore and with curiously tapering branches responsible for the common name, elephant tree. At one place and one place only has it ever been found in the United States—namely in a canyon at an elevation of about 4000 feet in the Baboquivari Mountains west of Tucson. The nearest Mexican specimen is many miles away. Plants do not leap such distances. It can be pretty safely taken for granted that the Arizona specimens were once joined by lines of communication to their fellows in Mexico.

What broke those lines and isolated these few specimens? Why did all the rest of this region become uninhabitable to them? In all probability the elephant tree will be as extinct in the United States as the elephant itself became so long ago. And it happens that this particular tree draws attention to itself because it has a very famous close relative in the East. To the Indians in Mexico it supplies a gum which they burn as incense. Its Eastern relative supplied the ancient peoples with their frankincense.

The story of how plants and animals were knowingly or unknowingly introduced by man into different parts of the earth is only part, and usually the clearest part, of a larger story—how the whole flora and fauna of a given region got to be what it is. By their own efforts plants and animals were advancing and retreating, colonizing and abandoning through all human history as well as through millions of years before there were any human beings to have a history. In many cases no one can do more than offer a more or less convincing guess concerning what actually happened. Until comparatively recently no one even asked the questions in any rational form.

For many years the late medieval herbalists went about northern Europe with a copy of an ancient Greek catalogue in their hands trying to identify in Germany or Sweden the flowers which the ancient author had found about the Mediterranean. They were loath to realize that theirs was what they would have thought of as a barbarous flora unknown to the ancients and no doubt loath also to face the fact that there was so much still to be learned. When the seventeenth and eighteenth centuries finally did realize something of the vast variety of living forms, they were concerned first of all to describe and list as many of them as possible, simply taking variety for granted. For them one sort of animal or plant lived in one place and another sort in another place because God had put them where they belonged. Each was a "special creation." If they all originated in the Garden of Eden then they must have been scattered as the sons of Noah were scattered in order that they might found the different races of mankind.

Consider how simple and how picturesque the situation was even as Linnaeus, child of an enlightened age, saw it. And he is delightfully explicit on the subject. There is, so he says, certainly more dry land now than there used to be. Probably Eden was situated upon a single small island while all the rest of the surface of the earth was under water. On this island, God crowded at least a specimen of every kind of plant or animal that now exists. Eden was a kind of Noah's Ark or, as he puts it, "a living museum of natural-history specimens." Linnaeus then concludes that Adam must have been the most fortunate of mankind because he had at hand everything which nature affords for use or pleasure, and that Adam's first duty in this "complete natural-history collection," was "to regard the Creator's work." It was—as Linnaeus does not add—too bad that when he named each according to its kind he did not realize the usefulness of the binomial system.

At other times even Linnaeus was somewhat troubled by the question whether two plants or animals which differed only slightly had, nevertheless, been to just that degree distinct since the fifth day of creation. He was, in other words, troubled by the need for a definition of "species," even if it was to be taken for granted that species had never changed. A century later Darwin's imagination and reason boggled at the assumption that God had created a special creature to live only on one rocky island in the Galapagos, a different one to live only on a neighboring island. But either God had gone to that pointless trouble or species were not fixed.

In any event, the flora and fauna of the world had to be described and catalogued, and then some theory of how the individual species of that flora and fauna had come into existence had to be formulated, before men could begin to study intelligently these various flora and fauna as self-contained entities or to ask how they had become established where they are. And it is a curious fact that biology began to be especially concerned with such questions at about the same time that sociology began to attract more and more attention among the students of the human animal. In some respects the cases are quite parallel. Ecology, the study of plant and animal associations, is merely the sociology of the whole plant and animal world. The biologist's shift of interest in the direction of ecological studies is parallel to the increasing tendency of students in another field to shift their interest from the study of individual men to the study of "society."

Something was said about all this when we raised the question how and when the cactus got to the Sonoran Desert. But the same question might be asked about any plant or animal anywhere—including, especially, every one that is fitted to live in arid country. When Tribulus terrestris was brought in and found that in many places things were quite to his liking, a member of the same mostly tropical and subtropical family—namely the creosote bush—was actually already the dominant shrub in regions drier than Tribulus really likes. How did it get here and why didn't Tribulus come with it?

We cannot do much more than guess, but probably the immediate ancestor of the creosote crossed some bridge which ceased to exist before the immediate ancestors of Tribulus had developed on the family tree. But the barriers once bridged, later impassable, do not by any means have to be oceans. One desert can, for instance, be isolated from another by an intervening barrier of moist fertility just as effectively as one moist area may be isolated from another by an intervening desert. When Tribulus was carried by man across the barriers it settled down happily to increase and multiply.

When the question why all animals and plants don't grow everywhere was first asked in scientific rather than mythological terms, the first answer was no doubt that some demand heat and that some won't tolerate it. Probably most men today would give an answer almost as simple. And of course it is true as far as it goes. But it is a long way from being a full answer. Some don't live where they very well could for the same reason that, for centuries, Europeans did not live in America—they had just never got there. Others don't because there are many things besides temperature to which some are absurdly sensitive.

Some of the subtler demands are only now beginning to be understood. For instance: some southern plants won't bloom and therefore can't reproduce themselves even in northern greenhouses, because the summer days are too long and give them too many hours of light; other plants will not flower except in isolated areas even within their geographical range, because they demand infinitesimal traces of certain chemical elements not everywhere present. That is probably why, a few miles south of Tucson and not far from the Mexican border, one will see in spring certain hillsides covered with yellow poppies, while another apparently identical hillside a few hundred yards away has none. As has only recently been demonstrated these poppies like a trace of copper, which happens to be present in some places and not in others.

Dates from the Near East will grow wonderfully here but in many places only if they are irrigated more than in their native desert habitat, because there is often less subsurface water in Arizona than in some parts of even the Sahara. And as we have already remarked, most of the palms which tourists admire as exotics along the Riviera are actually imports from California favored in Europe because they stand lower temperatures than most African palms like. By way of compensation, the tamarisks, which took firm hold here in the Southwest when planted by the

Forest Service to reduce erosion along the desert washes, are native to the same Mediterranean region to which California has sent its palms. Smyrna figs grow well in California but, as I have said before, wouldn't fruit until it was discovered that they had to have a certain wasp which not only had to be imported to please them, but which itself had to be given an otherwise useless scrub fig from the Near East upon which it depends during a part of its life cycle.

In a region of deserts broken up by mountains as our southwestern deserts are, such mountain or desert barriers are very important factors in controlling the distribution of animals as well as of plants, and "islands" of the one or the other are isolated long enough to begin to develop indigenous species very much as the isolated Galapagos Islands produced those which first puzzled and then enlightened Darwin. The best known case is that of the abert squirrel and the kaibab squirrel.

The first I see often at seven or eight thousand feet on the nearest mountain range. With the possible exception of the Sonoran fox squirrel, whom I have been lucky enough to glimpse within the few square miles where Arizona, New Mexico, and Old Mexico meet and where alone he consents to cross the border from Mexico, the abert is the handsomest squirrel I know: conspicuously larger than the familiar gray, brown-backed with an almost red saddle, with pointed ears emphasized by pointed tufts of hair, and with an exuberant tail part gray, part white. He is a mountain creature inhabiting a rather restricted area and south of the Grand Canyon he is just what I have described. North of the canyon his relative the kaibab squirrel with a pure white tail takes over completely. As usual there is the dispute—meaningless since evolution has been understood—whether the two are to be regarded as separate species or merely as separate varieties. But if the kaibab is not yet a separate species it is in the process of becoming one. Its race and that of the abert are separated by the great gash of the Canyon, running east and west, and they have been so separated ever since the Colorado River got well started on the cutting job which began a few million years ago. Perhaps, if man were to carry a few of each into the territory of the other they would interbreed and possibly eliminate the distinction. But unless man does so, or unless squirrels learn how to travel and to carry their food supplies with them, the aberts and the kaibabs may very well go on getting more and more different from one another just as races of men similarly isolated develop racial characteristics.

Workers in several different sciences are becoming more and more convinced that both the north temperate and the arctic climates are growing milder. A minor evidence is the way in which certain animals and birds—notably the 'possum, the turkey buzzard and the cardinal—are extending their range into New England. Here in the Southwest the same sort of thing is happening. The coati, comic relative of the raccoon, which used to belong only in Mexico and southward, is becoming increasingly common in southern Arizona. Even more striking is the case of the armadillo. Formerly known in the United States only from Texas and the Mexican frontier, it has spread during a mere seventy-five years into Oklahoma, Louisiana and even southern Arkansas. Though it is not, I am sorry to say, native here—sorry because I should like to know better a creature who is certainly not very smart but has many quaint habits, including the invariable habit of giving birth to its young in one or two sets of identical quadruplets. But even to know about the spread of the coati and the armadillo makes it easier to believe that tapirs and saber-toothed tigers really did once roam about what is now New York State.

"The buckeye," as Thoreau once oracularly declaimed, "does not grow in New England." But who knows? Some day it may. It was Thoreau also who confessed that, "I had no idea there was so much going on in Heywood's meadow." So there was and so there is in every meadow, and plain and mountain: things accomplished in a day, and others which require thousands of years before even their intention becomes apparent.

To say that something is as solid as the ground under one's feet is not to say much: that ground may be lifted miles into the air. Forests and grasslands and deserts flow like rivers. Stability, dominance and security are short-term words. We haven't a long enough view really to know what is even now in the process of happening to our earth or its populations, or what fateful changes are taking place—changes which may finally add up to something quite as tremendous as those which made the ice ages, or may even mark the end of a long geological epoch like the Paleozoic or the Mesozoic. Few stop to think what a small change in rainfall or a shift in a flora may mean even for their children or grandchildren. Like the city child who was not interested in cows because he got his milk from bottles, they forget how dependent we all are upon things over which we have no control. In the long run our boasted control of nature is a delusion. Ultimately all milk comes from cows. There is nothing that we can really get out of bottles.

THE VOICE OF THE DESERT

N I N E

and every single one of them is right

IT OUGHT TO BE OBVIOUS BY NOW THAT THERE ISN'T JUST one way to live in the desert. There must be at least thirty-five and, as Mr. Kipling once said of something else, "every single one of them is right," if you know how to do it. Animals and plants have been equally ingenious in finding them out and equally persistent in sticking to a given way once it has shown that it will work.

In every case the central problem remains the same: How to get water, how to keep it when you have got it, and how to get along with the minimum gettable and keepable. It has been demonstrated that only one animal has the ability to get along without water. None of the plants can manage without any external source whatsoever. But the plants have been most ingenious in the variety of the less radical solutions which they have worked out.

After all, they can't go looking for anything. They must live or die in the situation to which it has pleased God to call them. And like all creatures except an occasional man, they will go to great lengths in order to live. Legendary tales notwithstanding, even the scorpion does not commit suicide. Even if he wanted to he couldn't do it in the fashion legend long attributed to him, because scorpions are immune to their own poison. It is even harder to imagine a plant saying to itself, "Life just isn't worth living." Many a desert seed falls on stony ground and quite a few of them get along quite well anyway.

One of the oddest facts is that even within a group as strongly marked as the cacti, certain species have developed characteristic methods quite different from those usually employed by their relatives. Most of them, like the saguaro, have rather shallow root systems which means that they take up water only at rare intervals and store it in the thick stem. But one of the most beautiful as well as improbable of the desert cacti—the one which Mexicans call reina de la noche, or queen of the night— prefers a radically different method.

This striking plant stores very little water in the stem. In fact, it couldn't do so very effectively because the stem, though commonly three feet long and sometimes even six, is usually less than an inch in diameter and during most of the year it is quite dry, indeed to all appearances entirely dead. In that state it is so inconspicuous that I must have passed one established a foot or two from my roadway hundreds of times before I saw it. Yet once a year, usually in June or July, the queen suddenly opens lush, tropical-looking flowers that are pure white, six inches or more across, and heavily fragrant. Tannhäuser's pilgrim staff looked hardly less promising and produced less extravagant blossoms. Of what sin the queen of the night announces forgiveness I do not know, but since the miracle occurs so frequently I like to think that it may be Adam's and the share all of us have in it. At least the rainbow itself is no more surprising.

Though several blooms appear on one plant and sometimes successively, each opens in the evening and usually closes next morning. A good many different cacti are familiarly known as "night-blooming cereuses" but this is the only one which grows wild in Arizona. Moreover, the astonishing plant prefers very arid situations—often where nothing else except the unkillable creosote bush will grow. And the moment it chooses to come to life is one when the ground is usually dry as powder, not after a rainy season but toward the end of the driest of the year. What is its secret?

Dig one up and the answer is obvious. The two or three slender, dry, wand-like stems grow from the top of a huge tuber rather like an oversized turnip. The whole aboveground part of the plant can hardly weigh more than a few ounces, yet the tuber is sometimes enormous and frequently weighs between five and fifteen pounds. How many years it takes to grow to this size I do not know, but it must be many. Yet this peculiar plant's solution of the problem of how to live in the desert is plainly a practical one. Like the saguaro it takes up water when it can get it, but instead of storing what has been taken in a massive stem, it stores it underground where loss by evaporation must be even less. And when the time comes to bloom in the midst of an absolute drought, it is independent of prevailing conditions. It simply draws upon its private stock. Nor does it, the poet notwithstanding, "waste its sweetness on the desert air." When a blossom is fragrant that usually means that it needs some insect to pollinate it. When the blossom is white and opens at night that means that some night-flying insect is being invited. And you may be sure that it will accept the invitation. Before summer is over many of the stems of the queen will bear largish, pulpy red "pears" much like those of the commonest cactus.

If any reader happens to wonder just how well all the devices for economizing water really work, how efficient they really are, some very good answers can be given. We know that desert plants survive and flourish. But how much do their special mechanisms contribute to this survival? It happens that studies have been made on the saguaro, and those which compare it with the date palm, cultivated commercially in the saguaro belt, are especially impressive.

The date palm is not especially good at economizing water. Where it grows in the old-world deserts, in the Sahara for example, it can do so only where there is abundant subsurface moisture, and when natives want to establish a new grove they not only have to plant the young trees deep, but also to water them until the roots have had time to grow much deeper still. Here in Arizona, where such abundant subsurface water is not available, even the mature trees have to be irrigated, though of course saguaros which are growing nearby get no such pampering. Measurement of the moisture lost by evaporation in the course of a day makes the difference between the one and the other no mystery. The date palm may transpire five hundred quarts of water in twenty-four hours; a twelve-foot saguaro as little as one-fiftieth of one quart, or approximately one twenty-five thousandths as much. Obviously, if you are a plant and are going to live in the desert, leaflessness, succulence, a wax-coated skin and thorns to reduce the circulation of desiccating air all pay off.

But why should the saguaro adopt one device and the queen of the night another? The two must be quite closely related. It is not merely that both are cacti. They actually belong to the same genus of the cactus family and the structure of the stems with, in each case, longitudinal ridges extending along their entire length, is similar. The saguaro has taken advantage of this structure by making the ridges serve as the high edges of the accordion pleats which open to increase the volume when water is available. The queen of the night takes only very minor advantage of this feature and expands its root into a huge tuber instead.

The different devices adopted become even more interesting when you realize that other plants, not at all related and certainly having a very different evolutionary history, have independently recognized the same possibility of which the queen of the night took advantage. A good example is the common finger gourd of the desert, which runs for long distances over the ground or clambers over a shrub if it can find one.

Now the gourd family, or at least that genus with which

we are concerned, is principally tropical or subtropical and has supplied the pumpkins and squashes of the vegetable garden. There are no wild species native to the eastern United States and those which are cultivated are mostly annuals which require a good deal of moisture and have quite ordinary root systems. The finger gourd of the desert looks like a typical member of the group, with yellow pumpkin-like flowers and striped hard-shelled fruits three or four inches in diameter, quite similar to those often grown in the East for ornament. But come upon one, as I happened to do not long ago, which has been torn by a torrential summer rain from its bed beside a wash, and you will be amazed by a tuber weighing eight or ten pounds. Without leaves or stems it might be anything. In fact I did not know what my specimen was until I had planted it in my garden and got, a few weeks later, the unmistakable palmated leaves with which I had been long familiar without guessing from what an imposing root they came. In fact this gourd tuber looks quite a bit like that of the night-blooming cactus.

The necessity for some special adaptation is obvious. Gourds need a long growing season to mature their fruits. Moreover, their leaves are thin and watery, adapted neither for storing nor for holding water as the succulent plants do. Under desert conditions they could not hope to have soil moisture available during the whole of that long growing season. Hence the great tank below ground which can be drawn upon both to get a start in early summer and then, after the short period of midsummer rain, to carry on through hot, dry late August, September and October.

Clearly the queen of the night and the finger gourd hit

upon this method of survival, or rather of flourishing, quite independently. Anthropologists have long disputed whether or not the use of the same tool or instrument, say the throwing stick or the bow, in widely separated parts of the world must mean that there was at some time some contact between the ancestors of the one ethnic group and the other. But there can be no such question here. Plant families have spread across vast distances and they carry their hereditary characteristics with them. But they have no cultural traditions which can be communicated. The cactus can't teach the gourd. And when the same device has been invented by different plant groups there can be only one possible explanation. To any problem in chemistry or mechanics there are a limited number of possible solutions. Their number is fixed by the nature of things. And many, perhaps all, of that limited number of possible solutions have been hit upon again and again.

Nevertheless, there remains a harder question. Since there are so often several possible solutions, why has one plant or animal accepted one and another plant or animal another quite different? Why, to take an example, didn't the gourd become succulent above ground as so many plants of so many different families did when they adapted themselves to desert conditions?

Perhaps the answer would sometimes be clear if we could trace every step in the organism's history and see precisely how or under what aspects the problem presented itself to each plant or animal. But even so, the answer would probably not always be forthcoming. Something in the given nature of an individual species probably predisposes it to one solution rather than another.

This fact is one which students of evolution and genetics

have only comparatively recently been coming to recognize. Formerly it had often been rather casually taken for granted that all living things were equally and almost limitlessly plastic. They could vary in all directions. Environment, using natural selection as a method, was the only thing which determined what the final result would be. But certainly it is all neither so simple nor so one-sided a process as that. On the contrary, it now looks as though an individual species was often capable of developing in one direction and not in the other. Perhaps even the possibility of growing tubers was inherent in some and the possibility of developing succulence was inherent in others long before they were called upon to do either.

This is only another of the many ways in which evolution, though it most certainly did take place, has come to seem in some respects more and more, rather than less and less, puzzling as detailed information has accumulated. It is also another of the many illustrations of the fact that nature, working in her still mysterious ways, has worked better than she would have worked if man had been able to impose upon her the uniformity and efficiency which he seems to be coming more and more to desire.

This world would be a far less interesting as well as a far less varied place, if every problem which faces either plants or men was always solved in the same way. Thoreau remarked that he would like to have as many different kinds of men as possible. Fewer and fewer seem to agree with him. But it certainly looks as though nature wanted as many different kinds of living things as she could produce. And she pursues her love of variety even down to the smallest detail. If one beetle has twelve spots, she is pretty certain to make another with fifteen—and she is

almost as profuse in the desert. Water storage in a thick
stem works very well not only for the saguaro but also for
the great and very common barrel cactus, which, as I have
said before, really does hold enough water in its pulp to
save a human life in desperate cases. But that is no reason
why gourds and the queen of the night shouldn't go in for
underground tubers instead. Thus nature:

> . . . *fulfills herself in many ways*
> *Lest one good custom should corrupt the world.*

Most people whose experience has been limited to cultivated flowers and vegetables think a seed is something
you put into the ground, water a little if necessary and con-
fidently expect to come up. But a desert seed, like everything else about a desert plant, is peculiar. Plant it carefully, water it or not as you please, wait patiently and,
four times out of five, nothing at all happens. Dig it up
six months or even a year later and, as often as not, it
looks precisely as it did when you put it in the ground. In
fact it does not look as though it had been planted.

Newcomers who have had this experience—and I was
one of them—feel aggrieved. Native plants, they think,
ought to grow easily. They have been seen flourishing unattended in the most unpromising-looking spots. What
perversity has induced them to refuse to grow where you
want them to?

Actually, of course, and even in temperate climates,
wild plants are often much more difficult to grow than
tame ones. One of the reasons why the latter are cultivated is just that they are, or have been trained to be, relatively undemanding. And that really ought not surprise

anybody, since the same thing is true of domestic animals. It is a lot easier to keep a chicken or a canary in New England, where neither is native, than it would be to keep a chickadee, however many hundreds of the latter may be flourishing in the neighborhood. But what is to some extent true of many wild plants is especially true of the desert species. Beginning to live in the desert is, if anything, even more difficult than living there once you have got started. Many kinds of plants as well as animals can do it, but they have to do it in their own way.

As usual the number one difficulty for a chance seedling is created by the shortage of water except during the short wet periods. Most desert plants produce their seed at the end of a rainy season which is followed by a long drought. Obviously if the seeds fell to the ground and germinated in the possibly still damp earth they would, shortly after, be burned up. Some method had to be devised to prevent them from behaving in any such imprudent fashion. In the California and the Mexican deserts the problem is relatively simple because there is only one wet season, that of winter rains in the one and of summer rains in the other. But in southern Arizona it is complicated still further by the fact that there are two—in midsummer and midwinter. And since some plants do most of their growing after the winter rains and some after the summer, they have to be careful not to come up during the wrong wet period.

One way of getting around this difficulty is simply to refuse to come up at all except after one year (or perhaps two or three years) has passed. And that can be arranged by taking advantage of a trick which pharmacists have recently learned to play when they want to delay the action of some pill for a certain number of hours after it is taken: you coat it with some substance which will require a known number of hours to dissolve. Many desert seeds learned this trick many thousands of years ago. They are covered with a layer of wax which prevents the absorption of water until it has worn away and it wears away after an appropriate time. The beautiful shrub, Acacia constricta, which bears pompons of yellow flowers in spring is one such. The seeds are rather small, black and obviously waxy. Under natural conditions they will not germinate in less than a year's time. But if you cut through the outer coat, they will begin to grow immediately in damp earth.

I happen, however, to have a more intimate personal acquaintance with an even stranger plant, the coral bean. In this climate it is a smallish bush whose stems look dry and lifeless during most of the year. Like the queen of the night and the ocotillo it makes a specialty of blooming at the moment when it appears quite incapable of anything of the sort, and in early spring, after the winter rain, its bare stem breaks forth with bright compact masses of brilliant red flowers each some two inches long. Usually it waits until after the summer rains, six weeks or two months after it has bloomed, before it bothers to put forth the leaves which it drops again very early in the fall. Meanwhile, pods, much like those of the string bean and often well over a foot long, have been forming. By autumn they have split half-open to reveal a row of large beans, bright red in color, obviously waxy, and as hard as stones. In Mexico they are made into necklaces and they last indefinitely.

Innocently to plant one is to risk losing one's faith in the seed as a symbol of resurrection, or at least to suspect that these particular seeds are waiting for the last trump.

It is said that two or three years is the normal time for them to lie dormant, but I have never had the patience to discover and all I know is that six months after one was planted in sand and kept moist, nothing whatever had happened to alter its appearance. When I dug it up it still looked as though it were waiting to be made into a necklace. Yet, as I also know from experience, it is easy to trick them because the delay is merely the result of a simple mechanical device. With a file I scratched a line a few millimeters long through the wax and the hard outer skin. When I planted this bean it came up in just eight days and because I gave it the water it would not have got in nature at that season, I hope that it will produce seeds of its own a few years from now. It is already nearly a foot high and looks very flourishing.

But why should some seeds, like those of the bean, remain dormant not merely for one but for two or three years? That question I have never heard raised but I can make what sounds like a pretty good guess. In the desert there are not infrequent years unfavorable even for desert plants. During such years certain root perennials do not even come up and obviously it would be very unlikely that a seedling could establish itself at such a time. If one whole crop of coral beans was fated to germinate and die during such a year, it would obviously be a serious blow to the species in that region. But if some remained dormant for two and some for three years, the chance that one group or the other would ultimately produce successful plants would obviously be greatly increased. I mean to test this theory by planting a number in the same place to see if they come up in successive years. But this book will probably be published before I have the answer.

That the coral bean's reliance on as simple a mechanical device as the waxy coating works well, seems to be demonstrated by the fact that the plants are quite common in rocky canyons at moderate altitudes and their conspicuous scarlet flowers add a brilliant touch to the early summer landscape at a time when most spring flowers are past and those of late summer have not yet appeared. Nevertheless, many other plants prefer to depend instead upon the subtler operations of biochemistry. There is no visible reason, only a chemical one, why the seeds refuse to come up except at the one time a year when they can establish themselves.

In many parts of the world many plants solve their usually simpler problem in a similar way. Many a wild annual drops its seeds by midsummer when the soil is both warm and damp, but the seeds refuse to grow until the following spring when they will have before them a season of warmth long enough to permit them to come to maturity. Sometimes their secret is that certain necessary chemical preliminaries to growth are not complete when the seed falls but take place while it is apparently dormant. Sometimes it is that a winter's cold is necessary before the chemistry is right for growth. "Unless the seed die . . ." And dying in these cases means being chilled as well as dried out.

In southern Arizona things are less simple. There is the very long hot summer but there are only two very short wet seasons. Some plants flourish just after the first one, which ends about as spring begins; others, during and after the brief midsummer rains. The seeds of both lie in the ground all winter and those of the first sort during most of at least one summer as well. But the seeds of spring flowers won't sprout until the following spring, and the seeds of midsummer plants won't sprout until the following summer. Yet in neither case is it merely a matter of how long they must remain dormant. The spring group waits until it is wet but cool, the summer group until it is wet and warm. Elaborate experiments carried on some years ago at the now disbanded Carnegie Desert Laboratory established not only the general fact but the critical temperatures. For most of the winter ephemerals the optimum temperature for germination is 60 to 65 degrees, for the summer ephemerals between 80 and 90. Most will do fairly well within a range of 5 to 8 degrees above or below the optimum. That leaves a margin of about 5 to 10 degrees between the highest temperature at which the seeds of the spring flowers will grow and the lowest acceptable to the summer ones. It seems a narrow margin of safety where so much is at stake. But it is not too narrow to work very successfully. No feature of the desert is more striking than the spring carpet of flowers which covers large areas with thousands of blossoms. Yet the seed from which each sprang had to resist, during the whole previous summer, any temptation to germinate when the ground was moist and (one would have supposed) pleasantly warm. It had to wait until moisture with coolness proved that spring, not summer, had come.

It happens that I am writing this chapter in midwinter, and on the table beside me are a number of containers which represent my successes and my failures in various attempts to deceive desert seeds into believing that the time for their resurrection is right. One of the most con-

spicuous successes is a little blue wild morning glory
which normally begins to grow in early summer and cannot be very exacting because it is found in a variety of
situations and, unlike many plants of this region, at altitudes ranging all the way from fifteen hundred to five or
six thousand feet. Room temperature must have been acceptable and it is actually blooming in mid-December, thus
demonstrating that in another respect it is far from cranky.

Quite recently experiments have demonstrated that
many plants will grow if temperature and moisture are
right but will stubbornly refuse to bloom unless they get
light for the correct number of hours per day—and that
means neither too many nor too few. This explains, as we
noted earlier, why some southern plants will seem to
flourish in northern greenhouses but refuse nevertheless
to bloom. Asters and chrysanthemums hold off blossoming
until late summer or fall no matter how soon they are
planted, because they want a rather short day and won't
flower even at the appropriate season if so much as an
electric bulb convinces them that long summer days are
still prevailing. My morning glory is getting fewer hours
of light than it would get in nature but it is obliging with
very pretty little blossoms nonetheless. Obviously not a
crank.

My most conspicuous failures probably lie among those
plants which are triggered by temperature. Perhaps if I
had thermostatically controlled heat they too could be persuaded that it was spring or summer as the case might be;
but I haven't. Often some other specific conditions can't
be met, as I am beginning to suspect must be the case
with an unusually handsome wild four o'clock which

grows from a large tuberous root and flourished wonderfully last summer after it had been transplanted to my little wild garden.

It produced abundant seed. Yet, though I tried various tricks, not one seed would grow during the winter. Finally I put some in a refrigerator for two months and planted one after it had been permitted to enjoy an artificial hibernation. Not only did it come up promptly, but it seems to be healthy and promises well for another summer. Perhaps all it needed was the assurance that a winter had passed and that it could therefore count upon six or eight months to get a good start.

All these, I recognize, will seem very mild amusements to some. But there is no accounting for tastes and I greatly prefer them to many of the others which most of my fellows choose. At least they serve to remind me how wrong those early romantics were when they feared that knowledge would destroy that "sense of wonder" they cherished as though it were a very fragile thing. The wax coat over my coral bean "explains" why it will not grow in nature until a year or two has passed. But what will explain the explanation?

The more one comes to understand the mechanisms, the more amazing becomes the fact that they exist. And one must be very easily satisfied if one is satisfied to be told that they "evolved." With every passing year it becomes more difficult to understand why or how evolution operates. Fact after new fact proves that the whole process is much more complicated than Darwin imagined, and that the great mystery is not that changing conditions called for new adaptations but that the power to respond to the demands in certain ways, but not in others, was potential in living organisms. It is not ignorance but knowledge which is the mother of wonder.

Since seeds are among the most wonderful things in a world of wonder, it is not surprising that, ever since Old Testament times, they have been used in analogies and metaphors. The Preacher and the Psalmist are both sound enough—"In the morning sow thy seed" and "He that goeth forth and weepeth, bearing precious seed, shall doubtless come again with rejoicing, bringing his sheaves with him." So too are the Gospel authors: "Unless the seed die . . ." and "Some seeds fell by the wayside." But what of the modern preachers who invoke the seed to "prove" that man is immortal? Are seeds really that?

Unfortunately for the analogy they are not. They are only astonishingly durable and they prove only how low life can lie and how long it can endure. Doubtless the coral bean which frequently waits several years before it begins to grow could still germinate after a good many years had passed, though after just how many I have no idea. And as every gardener knows, the longer you keep a packet of seeds, the smaller the proportion of them that will ever grow. Hence it is obvious that the power to resume life after dormancy varies with the individual even within a given species. As an experiment I planted several hundred seeds of wild plants which had lain in a desk drawer for at least twenty years and only two sprouted.

Nevertheless, controlled experiments do prove that some may remain alive for much longer than that. In 1879 a botanist at Michigan State College filled twenty bottles with weed seed and buried the bottles eighteen inches below ground. From time to time they have been taken up and a few of the seeds planted. In 1950, or seventy-one years after the seeds were gathered, some from an evening primrose, a yellow dock and a moth mullen came up.

Botanists agree that the layman's favorite story about the flourishing of the wheat recovered from an Egyptian mummy, or of the corn from an Indian cliff dwelling has never been authenticated and until comparatively recently they were inclined to be very skeptical of all alleged cases of viability which endured for centuries. But in 1923 the most extraordinary case ever definitely established made the mummy stories seem again within the range of remotely possible fact. In that year a Japanese botanist found in a bog in Manchuria the seeds of a species of lotus extinct in that region. When he planted them they grew, and he guessed that they were at least several hundred years old. But we now know that he was overconservative. Tested by the new radioactive carbon method, they turned out to have been produced by a plant which was growing approximately one thousand years ago. Seeds are almost certainly not immortal. But they are certainly more enduring than scientists used to believe.

TEN

first on the mountain top

ARIZONA IS NOT ALL DESERT, BECAUSE SO MUCH OF IT IS mountain. Scores of separate ranges, each with a name of its own, are sprinkled here and there, and in the southern part of the state they often rise abruptly from the desert floor itself. In fact it is nearly impossible to move anywhere so far away from them that the horizon is not ringed around with peaks.

Many were formed at about the same time as the main body of the Rockies, many others are volcanic cores belched up in more recent times. And all, though especially of course the ancient ones, are less high than they once were. The desert valley is usually "fill" washed off from the mountain's mass. Around the bases of the mountains is piled the coarser debris in which they are slowly burying themselves. These "talus slopes," as such collections of boulders and large stones are called, are among the most distinctive features of the landscape, because only where precipitation is low do even the larger fragments from a decaying mountain remain so close to the slopes down which they tumbled. Even so, many peaks in the southern deserts still rise seven to nine thousand feet above sea level, five or six above the deserts upon which they are based. Many are higher than any summit east of the Mississippi.

All these mountains are relatively dry because higher mountains lie between them and the seas from which moist winds blow. But they are cooler than the deserts and they also get more rain, squeezing the last moisture out of clouds which have managed to pass over the barriers to the west or from moist air coming from the south and leaving still less for the flat lands in their rain shadow. From a distance their flanks look almost bare, but near the more humid summits they are often crowned with pines.

These mountains do much more than please the eye. Every thousand feet means a perceptible change in temperature and rainfall so that the mountains are responsible for the fact, so surprising to the newcomer, that Arizona is astonishingly rich in the number of different plants, animals and birds native there. Yet most dwellers in the larger towns are little more aware than town dwellers in other lands usually are of the biota of which they are a part. To them the mountains, if they mean anything,

mean a drive along one of the automobile roads which
lead up a few of them—in summer, to cooler regions; in
winter, to snow half an hour away from a sunny 70 degrees in town.

But to the student of nature they mean several distinct
worlds and the possibility of moving from one to the other
more quickly and easily than is possible in any but a relatively few regions of the earth. Within a distance of a
few hundred miles one may move from a subtropical desert near sea level at Yuma to the summit of the San Fran-
cisco Peaks whose more than twelve-thousand-foot altitude
carries the visitor into a region where some of the plants
are those which grow within the Arctic Circle.

Even more spectacular because one need travel only tens
rather than hundreds of miles is the journey from the
Sonoran Desert around Tucson to the pine and fir forests
which correspond to those found near sea level in southern Canada. To travel a thousand feet upward is, so far
as climate is concerned, the approximate equivalent of
traveling six hundred miles northward. Because this fact is
so spectacularly demonstrated in Arizona and eastern California, studies there were largely responsible for the conception of Life Zones which was formulated a little more
than half a century ago by C. Hart Merriam and has
now become fundamental in ecology.

Probably the most striking illustration to be found in
America of what this zoning means is supplied by the
now famous Mount San Jacinto in southeastern California. It rises from its base near Palm Springs and almost
at sea level to nearly ten thousand feet. The eastern slope is
so steep that eight thousand feet of altitude is gained in
only three linear miles, so that zones ranging from the

lower Sonoran at the bottom to the Boreal at the summit are compressed within this incredibly short distance. Ecologically one travels nearly five thousand miles while actually traveling only three, and the floral bands representing each zone are preposterously narrow.

Animals are less rigidly confined to their special zones than plants, and birds somewhat less than animals. Even so, the fauna as well as the flora of a mountain slope often tends to be confined very strikingly to particular zones. In the mountains around Tucson, for example, one is not likely to find jays below the level where the evergreen oaks grow, or to find a gilded flicker much higher than where these same oaks are just beginning to take over. Some birds migrate upward a short distance in summer, downward in winter, thus saving themselves the long journeys taken by others who must change latitudes because they have not convenient facilities for merely changing altitude instead. Many animals also stick quite closely to their own zone on the slope of a mountain, less because they are sensitive to temperature than because it is only in a particular zone that their food plants flourish. One will find them isolated by desert lowlands or by peaks from their fellows, whom one will find again at the same altitude on another range. Thus a map of any considerable mountain with the zones marked in color makes a sort of biological pousse-café. Carried blindfold to an unfamiliar region even a very moderately knowing student would need only a glance about him to guess pretty accurately at what altitude he found himself.

To climb the east flank of San Jacinto is a bit of an undertaking but the most sedentary can be shown what a life zone is from the window of a car as it climbs the fine motor road in the Catalinas near Tucson to a height of nearly eight thousand feet.

If we begin just northeast of the city limits we will find ourselves on a flat plain composed of sandy clay. For at least several hundred feet below the surface it is a hard-packed "fill" from the mountains, not very pervious to water and supporting little conspicuous vegetation except for the omnipresent creosote bush and the occasional low mesquite tree. Most birds do not very much favor it, though the road runner, the irascible-looking curved bill thrasher and the exuberant cactus wren are common, and you may see also the crested, jet black, phainopepla perched at the top of a mesquite after the manner of the flycatcher kind. Jack rabbits lope off into the distance and little round-tailed ground squirrels, their plumeless tails high in the air, dash madly across the road.

Suddenly, almost at a line which could be drawn, the whole appearance changes. A solitary saguaro raises its arms. Then two, then a dozen. Between them the green-trunked paloverde spreads its equally green limbs and twigs or, if this is early spring, is almost obscured in its yellow blossoms. Prickly pears and cholla cactus are scattered about in profusion. But what has happened? Why have these things suddenly taken over? The difference in altitude between the creosote desert and this succulent desert is hardly perceptible.

Most of the answer lies underfoot. Offhand one would say that the soil looks less suitable for plant life than what one has just left. In fact its gravelly surface appears most unpromising. And for a good many feet below the surface, gravelly is exactly what it is because this is the region of the coarser detritus from the mountains. But when a rain falls on this porous ground, it soaks in, providing abundant water for at least a few hours, or long enough for it to be snatched by shallow, wide-spreading roots. Certain birds, including especially the beautiful gilded flicker, like it better than the creosote flats and so does the Harris ground squirrel who looks rather like a chipmunk with an unusually fluffy tail and who puts in a frequent appearance. Within a mile or two after the first saguaro one is definitely mounting the talus slope and one is definitely in the midst of what is called the succulent desert.

Soon the road is climbing steeply, the ancient walls of the not-yet-eroded mountain on one side, on the other a sheer drop of several hundred feet into the canyon cut by a stream which may now be dry but whose bed is followed by a serpentine line of cottonwoods, perhaps even of willows. Toward the upper limit of this zone ocotillos, which wave in spring their blood-red flowers, begin to appear. Then, somewhere about forty-five hundred feet, again on a line as sharp as that of the tree limit in colder climes, the saguaros stop.

Through at least the lower portions of the zone we have just passed, frost is less common than on the valley floor because the cold air from the heights flows off and collects in the valley below. Now, however, the influence of altitude begins to overweigh that of slope and the air grows cooler. The characteristic tree is now the evergreen oak, of which there is a bewildering number of species. Yuccas and agaves, or century plants, have taken over as the most conspicuous of smaller perennials. The Harris ground squirrel is seen no more. In his place is the rich brown cliff chipmunk—a very good "indicator" animal because he seldom wanders down into his cousin's country. This, then, is the upper Sonoran zone at its most typical, and it continues upward for two thousand feet or more. Only toward its upper limit is snow likely to lie even a few days at a time in winter.

Now junipers are scattered more frequently among the oaks and then, almost before we can be aware what has happened, we have plunged into the pine forests of the transition zone. Temperature is partly responsible for the change but rainfall is perhaps more important. At sixty-five hundred feet some twenty inches, nearly twice what the desert gets, may fall and, what is almost equally important, a considerable portion of it may fall as snow to cover the ground for weeks at a time and to soak slowly in as it melts. The Arizona pine—barely distinguishable from the better-known ponderosa yellow pine—may lift its head a hundred feet, casting a deep shade upon the needle-carpeted floor precisely as the evergreen forests do in northern regions. And near the upper limit of this zone there are many firs. The abert squirrel, one of the largest and handsomest of its tribe, pricks up pointed ears and flourishes the extravagant panache of grayish tail as it searches for edible cones. Large flocks of the steel blue Arizona jays sail screaming from tree to tree. And quietly among the branches the little pigmy nuthatch goes about its business as much at home as it is in the evergreen forests of the state of Washington.

Here is nothing to remind one of the sunny desert not half an hour away by car. Not a plant or an animal would know how to live in the desert. Most do not even know that the desert exists. The wandering animal has always turned back at the edge of his familiar environment. Seeds of plants which fell over the line perished. Only man is limitlessly mobile. Only he creates everywhere the environment which he must have. The jay and the squirrel hide acorns and nuts for the winter. But they have never learned the trick of establishing food bases in inhospitable territory, much less how to travel with, as Thoreau puts it, "shiploads of preserved meats" and, at journey's end, with the empty cans "piled sky-high for a sign."

Any mountain range in southern Arizona will provide the opportunity for a journey in altitude and any will tell two stories. The first is this life-zone story of what is; the second, almost as clear, is the story of what was. All the mountains were once not only higher than they are, but also more barren—originally, indeed, completely so. Even now the soil is usually thin and great rocky peaks jut through it. Every plant and every animal that lives there descends from a race of colonists and each of the successive waves of colonization prepared the way for the one which came after. There could be no squirrels until there were oaks or pines to supply them with food. There could be no oaks or pines until generations of smaller plants had grown and died to make the soil in which they grow. But these smaller plants could not have grown upon the bare rocks when they were first lifted high in the air some hundreds of millions of years ago. How did it all start? By what steps did life conquer the forbidding lifeless steeps?

Before I leave the heights I usually like to look again at the answer to this question. And the process is still going on. Many bare rocks are still completely bare unless one looks closely. And what is happening on these al-

most bare rocks is what happened on others so long ago
that that bare rock is now overlaid with pine forest.

The secret lies, of course, in that thin, dry-looking en-
crustation, gray or greenish or yellow, which covers part
of the surface of many of even the barest rocks. The
casual eye takes it so for granted that it is hardly noticed.
And even when noticed it looks less like a living thing
than like some sort of sediment on, or exudation from,
the rock itself. Yet insignificant as it appears, it is an indispensable link. Only because it could grow there where
nothing else had ever grown before, is the mountain ultimately carpeted with plants and clothed with forests.

No life seems dimmer than the life of these lichens.
They grow so slowly that some individuals may just possibly be among the longest-lived organisms on earth. They
also grow almost everywhere—on tree trunks and fences
as well as upon walls and boulders, from the steaming
tropics to the arctic tundra. They may even, so some
sober scientists think, grow on the greenish planet Mars
where no other organism we know anything about could
possibly survive. Almost the only places they do not thrive
are smoky industrial cities.

Everywhere they suggest life at its gentlest, most sub-
dued and most enduring. Nothing else except, perhaps,
the bacteria seems to ask so little in order to stay alive.
And slowly and persistently as they grow they seem to
grow to no purpose. They are so humble that even Thoreau was a little apologetic about his interest in them,
and they are so unpromising in appearance that it was not
until after Thoreau's day that the secret of their structure
and physiology was deciphered. Yet they were here millions of years before we were; they not improbably may

still be here millions of years after we are gone, and much that is here now would never have been here at all if they had not first colonized the inhospitable rocks.

At the summits of Arizona mountains several different species flourish but the most conspicuous, perhaps, is that which appears as a golden yellow blotch hugging the stone so tightly that from a few feet away it might well be mistaken for a vein of mineral. And even at close range it seems more part of the rock itself than of anything growing upon it.

Like all lichens, it is, oddly enough, not one plant but two, though that surprising fact was only rather recently discovered. All lichens seem so bafflingly featureless that Linnaeus, the first great classifier, did not know what to do with them and ended by putting them into a large pigeonhole with a lot of other odds and ends. The penetration of their secret had to wait for the perfection of the microscope. And what a strange secret it turned out to be!

No species of lichen is, strictly speaking, a species at all. In every case what we call a lichen turns out to be a fungus—something like the mould on bread—and an alga—something like the green threadlike scum on a pond—living together in close, mutually beneficial association. When the time comes for reproduction, nature sees to it that the partners shall start life again together. In many cases what happens is that a bit of the fungus and a bit of the alga break off together. The wind blows the dry fragment away and when it comes to rest in some suitable place the two organisms begin again to grow in partnership.

Many different species of fungi and of algae have been able to strike up this odd relationship and each different pair constitutes a different sort of lichen. Sometimes the alga can also be found in nature living on its own. The fungus seems always to have lost its power to survive in nature except as one half of a partnership. Less than a hundred years ago botanists first came to understand the strange situation and for a while some remained skeptical about it. But they were convinced when an experimenter succeeded in actually synthesizing a lichen. He grew the fungus and the alga separately. Then he brought them together to form a lichen different from either.

This is not, be it noted, a case of parasitism. One plant does not live off the other. What we have instead is one of the closest and most striking cases of symbiosis, of living together because living together is advantageous to both organisms. The fungus, having no green chlorophyll, cannot manufacture its own food from chemical substances and it gets its organic nourishment from the green alga which can. In return it protects the alga from drought and collects the chemicals which the alga can turn into assimilable food for both the partners. Competition and strife are not the only laws of life. The algae are among the oldest and most primitive of all living things. The evidence of very ancient rocks indicates that they were flourishing perhaps a billion years before any plant or animal capable of forming a clearly outlined fossil had appeared. Yet even an alga is able to cooperate as well as compete.

Man has consciously used lichens in various minor ways. One species furnishes a dye still used in the Highlands to color homespun. Another supplies the essential substance in the litmus paper of the chemist. On the northern tundras the so-called "reindeer moss," as important to grazing animals as grass in temperate climates, is really a lichen. So too is the "Iceland moss" which Eskimos eat. Still another species used as a food in southwest Asia in times of famine may have been the manna of the Old Testament. But the lichen's greatest service—one that man was long unaware of—was paving the way for all other plants.

Imagine a granite peak which some cataclysm has thrust up into the cold air. It is hard, and smooth and dead. No root could penetrate it or find nourishment if it did. Frost might crack and flake the surface in time, but it would still be incapable of sustaining even the humblest weed.

Presently the wind carries aloft the spore of a lichen which comes to rest on the bare surface. A little moisture is all it requires. It can cling to the bare surface without roots. It can live on the infinitesimal traces of ammonia and other chemicals in the air. It carpets the bare rock with a thin film of living matter. Some sorts can live even on glass and they have been known to damage church windows by eating their way into them!

Presently the lichen on the mountain top dies. But where life has been, other forms of life can establish themselves. Perhaps the spore of a moss comes next and is able to exist because of the less-than-paper-thick coating of organic matter left by the lichen. When the moss dies that coating will be considerably thicker. Some less humble plant—not improbably a fern—can grow there now. After it will come something else still larger.

Meanwhile, frost and the mild acids of the growing things have begun to break down the rock. It cracks and crumbles. Into the little pockets formed here and there the rain washes the remains of the lichen, the moss and the fern. They are mixed with the gravel and sand of the disintegrating granite. They are "humus," that all-important ingredient of all fertile soil, supplying food and moisture for the plants which grow in it.

Each larger herb or shrub adds its contribution to the humus. After thousands of years a great pine may be growing where nothing had grown before and where nothing could ever have grown if the lichen, which asks so little, had not come first. This process has taken place countless times in the past. It is following the same sequence of events today in countless places and one need only look about in any mountain region to see the various stages. Where the pine is was once a lichen. Where the lichen is may some day, perhaps millennia hence, be a pine.

It would be a rash man who would undertake to estimate very closely the age of one of the lichens growing on an Arizona peak or anywhere else. Unfortunately they produce no annual rings to be counted. They cannot even be dated by the new carbon isotope method because that method reveals only how long ago a thing died, not for how long it has been living. But one thing is certain. Many lichens grow very, very slowly and they must have taken a long time to reach the size attained by some individuals.

It is commonly said that the giant redwoods of California are the most ancient individual living organisms, and they are old enough. A fallen giant whose rings can be counted had lived for a little more than three thousand years. A still standing tree is almost certainly quite a bit older. But it has been suggested with some show of reason that certain very large individual lichens may be even older. Perhaps not the majestic tree but a humble lichen has lived through more history than any other growing thing.

When you see a large one on a boulder you can at least feel sure that the boulder has not been much disturbed for a very long time. No wonder that a rolling stone gathers no moss. It would have to gather some lichens first. And lichens take a lot of time to prepare a stone to grow moss or anything else.

Before I start my downward journey to the warm desert again I cast a backward look at the golden lichen patiently spreading over the rock. It carries the reassuring suggestion that nature is preparing for a long future. The acorn is planted for the sake of the oak to come. No one that I ever heard of cared to look far enough ahead to plant a lichen in the conviction that some day a pine would grow there. Nature did, and her faith was justified. Perhaps it will be again.

E L E V E N

love in the desert

THE ANCIENTS CALLED LOVE "THE MOTHER OF ALL THINGS," but they didn't know the half of it. They did not know, for instance, that plants as well as animals have their love life and they supposed that even some of the simpler animals were generated by sunlight on mud without the intervention of Venus.

Centuries later when Chaucer and the other medieval poets made "the mystic rose" a euphemism for an anatomical structure not commonly mentioned in polite society, they too were choosing a figure of speech more appropriate than they realized, because every flower really is a group of sex organs which the plants have glorified while the animals—surprisingly enough, as many have observed —usually leave the corresponding items of their own anatomy primitive, unadorned and severely functional. The ape, whose behind blooms in purple and red, represents the most any of the higher animals has achieved along this line and even it is not, by human standards, any great aesthetic success. At least no one would be likely to maintain that it rivals either the poppy or the orchid.

In another respect also plants seem to have been more aesthetically sensitive than animals. They have never tolerated that odd arrangement by which the same organs are used for reproduction and excretion. Men, from St. Bernard to William Butler Yeats, have ridiculed or scorned it and recoiled in distaste from the fact that, as Yeats put it, "love has pitched his mansion in / The place of excrement." As a matter of fact, the reptiles are the only backboned animals who have a special organ used only in mating. Possibly—though improbably, I am afraid—if this fact were better known it might be counted in favor of a generally unpopular group.

All this we now know and, appropriately enough, much of it—especially concerning the sexuality of plants—was first discovered during the eighteenth-century Age of Gallantry. No other age would have been more disposed to hail the facts with delight and it was much inclined to expound the new knowledge in extravagantly gallant terms. One does not usually think of systematizers as given to rhapsody, but Linnaeus, who first popularized the fact that plants can make love, wrote rhapsodically of their nuptials:

The petals serve as bridal beds which the Great Creator has so gloriously arranged, adorned with such noble bed curtains and perfumed with so many sweet scents, that the bridegroom there may celebrate his nuptials with all the greater solemnity. When the bed is thus prepared, it is time for the bridegroom to embrace his beloved bride and surrender his gifts to her: I mean, one can see how testiculi *open and emit* pulverem genitalem, *which falls upon* tubam *and fertilizes* ovarium.

In England, half a century later, Erasmus Darwin, distinguished grandfather of the great Charles, wrote even more exuberantly in his didactic poem, "The Loves of the Plants," where all sorts of gnomes, sylphs and other mythological creatures benevolently foster the vegetable *affaires de coeur*. It is said to have been one of the best-selling poems ever published, no doubt because it combined the newly fashionable interest in natural history with the long standing obsession with "the tender passion" as expressible in terms of cupids, darts, flames and all the other clichés which now survive only in St. Valentine's Day gifts.

Such romantic exuberance is not much favored today when the seamy side is likely to interest us more. We are less likely to abandon ourselves to a participation in the joys of spring than to be on our guard against "the pathetic fallacy" even though, as is usually the case, we don't know exactly what the phrase means or what is "pathetic" about the alleged fallacy. Nevertheless, those who consent, even for a moment, to glance at that agreeable surface of things with which the poets used to be chiefly concerned will find in the desert what they find in every other spring, and they may even be aware that the hare, which here also runs races with itself, is a good deal fleeter than any Wordsworth was privileged to observe in the Lake Country.

In this warm climate, moreover, love puts in his appearance even before "the yonge sonne hath in the Ram his halfe cours y-ronne" or, in scientific prose, ahead of the spring equinox. Many species of birds, which for months have done little more than chirp, begin to remember their songs. In the canyons where small pools are left from some winter rain, the subaqueous and most mysterious of all spring births begins and seems to recapitulate the first morning of creation. Though I have never noticed that either of the two kinds of doves which spend the whole year with us acquire that "livelier iris" which Tennyson celebrated, the lizard's belly turns turquoise blue, as though to remind his mate that even on their ancient level sex has its aesthetic as well as its biological aspect. Fierce sparrow hawks take to sitting side by side on telegraph wires, and the Arizona cardinal, who has remained all winter long more brilliantly red than his eastern cousin ever is, begins to think romantically of his neat but not gaudy wife. For months before, he had been behaving like an old married man who couldn't remember what he once saw in her. Though she had followed him about, he had sometimes driven her rudely away from the feeding station until he had had his fill. Now gallantry begins to revive and he may even graciously hand her a seed.

A little later the cactus wren and the curved-bill thrasher will build nests in the wicked heart of the cholla cactus and, blessed with some mysterious impunity, dive through its treacherous spines. Somewhere among the creosote bushes, by now yellow with blossoms, the jack rabbit—

an unromantic looking creature if there ever was one—
will be demonstrating that she is really a hare, not a rabbit
at all, by giving birth to young furred babies almost ready
to go it alone instead of being naked, helpless creatures
like the infant cottontail. The latter will be born underground, in a cozily lined nest; the more rugged jack rabbit on the almost bare surface.

My special charge, the Sonoran spadefoot toad, will remain buried no one knows how many feet down for
months still to come. He will not celebrate his spring until
mid-July when a soaking rain penetrates deeply enough to
assure him that on the surface a few puddles will form.
Some of those puddles may just possibly last long enough
to give his tadpoles the nine or ten days of submersion
necessary, if they are to manage the metamorphosis which
will change them into toadlets capable of repeating that
conquest of the land which their ancestors accomplished
so many millions of years ago. But while the buried spadefoots dally, the buried seeds dropped last year by the little
six-week ephemerals of the desert will spring up and proceed with what looks like indecent haste to the business of
reproduction, as though—as for them is almost the case—
life were not long enough for anything except preparation
for the next generation.

Human beings have been sometimes praised and sometimes scorned because they fall so readily into the habit
of pinning upon their posterity all hope for a good life, of
saying, "At least my children will have that better life
which I somehow never managed to achieve." Even plants
do that, as I know, because when I have raised some of
the desert annuals under the unsuitable conditions of a
winter living room, they have managed, stunted and sickly

though they seemed, to seed. "At least," they seemed to say, "our species is assured another chance." And if this tendency is already dominant in a morning glory, human beings will probably continue to accept it in themselves also, whether, by human standards, it is wise or not.

As I write this another spring has just come around. With a regularity in which there is something pleasantly comic, all the little romances, dramas and tragedies are acting themselves out once more, and I seize the opportunity to pry benevolently.

Yesterday I watched a pair of hooded orioles—he, brilliant in orange and black; she, modestly yellow green—busy about a newly constructed nest hanging from the swordlike leaves of a yucca, where one would have been less surprised to find the lemon yellow cousin of these birds which builds almost exclusively in the yucca. From this paradise I drove away the serpent—in this case a three-foot diamondback rattler who was getting uncomfortably close to the nesting site—and went on to flush out of the grass at least a dozen tiny Gambel's quail whose male parent, hovering close by, bobbed his head plume anxiously as he tried to rally them again. A quarter of a mile away a red and black Gila monster was sunning himself on the fallen trunk of another yucca, and, for all I know, he too may have been feeling some stirring of the spring, though I can hardly say that he showed it.

From birds as brightly colored as the orioles one expects only gay domesticity and lighthearted solicitude. For that reason I have been more interested to follow the home life of the road runner, that unbird-like bird whom we chose at the beginning as a desert dweller par excellence. One

does not expect as much of him as one does of an oriole
for two good reasons. In the first place, his normal manner is aggressive, ribald and devil-may-care. In the second
place, he is a cuckoo, and the shirking of domestic respon-
sibilities by some of the tribe has been notorious for so
long that by some confused logic human husbands who
are the victims of unfaithfulness not only wear the horns
of the deer but are also said to be cuckolded. The fact remains, nevertheless, that though I have watched the developing domestic life of one road runner couple for
weeks, I have observed nothing at which the most critical
could cavil.

The nest—a rather coarse affair of largish sticks—was
built in the crotch of a thorny cholla cactus some ten feet
above the ground, which is rather higher than usual. When
first found there were already in it two eggs, and both of
the parent birds were already brooding them, turn and
turn about. All this I had been led to expect because the
road runner, unlike most birds, does not wait until all the
eggs have been laid before beginning to incubate. Instead
she normally lays them one by one a day or two apart and
begins to set as soon as the first has arrived. In other
words the wife follows the advice of the Planned Par-
enthood Association and "spaces" her babies—perhaps because lizards and snakes are harder to come by than insects, and it would be too much to try to feed a whole nest
full of nearly grown infants at the same time. Moreover,
in the case of my couple "self-restraint" or some other
method of birth control had been rigorously practiced and
two young ones were all there were.

Sixteen days after I first saw the eggs, both had hatched.
Presently both parents were bringing in lizards according

to a well-worked-out plan. While one sat on the nest to protect the young from the blazing sun, the other went hunting. When the latter returned with a catch, the brooding bird gave up its place, went foraging in its turn and presently came back to deliver a catch, after which it again took its place on the nest. One day, less than a month after the eggs were first discovered, one baby was standing on the edge of the nest itself, the other on a cactus stem a few feet away. By the next day both had disappeared.

Thus, despite the dubious reputation of the family to which he belongs, the road runner, like the other American cuckoos, seems to have conquered both the hereditary taint and whatever temptations his generally rascally disposition may have exposed him to. In this case at least, both husband and wife seemed quite beyond criticism, though they do say that other individuals sometimes reveal a not-too-serious sign of the hereditary weakness when a female will, on occasion, lay her eggs in the nest of another bird of her own species—which is certainly not so reprehensible as victimizing a totally different bird as the European cuckoo does.

Perhaps the superior moral atmosphere of America has reformed the cuckoo's habit and at least no American representative of the family regularly abandons its eggs to the care of a stranger. Nevertheless, those of us who are inclined to spiritual pride should remember that we do have a native immoralist, abundant in this same desert country and just as reprehensible as any to be found in decadent Europe—namely the cowbird, who is sexually promiscuous, never builds a home of his own and is inveterately given to depositing eggs in the nests of other birds. In his defense it is commonly alleged that his "antisocial conduct" should be excused for the same reason that such conduct is often excused in human beings—because, that is to say, it is actually the result not of original sin but of certain social determinants. It seems that long before he became a cowbird this fellow was a buffalo bird. And because he had to follow the wide ranging herds if he was to profit from the insects they started up from the grass, he could never settle down long enough to raise a family. Like Rousseau and like Walt Whitman, he had to leave his offspring (if any) behind.

However that may be, it still can hardly be denied that love in the desert has its still seamier side. Perhaps the moth, whom we have already seen playing pimp to a flower and profiting shamelessly from the affair, can also be excused on socio-economic grounds. But far more shocking things go on in dry climates as well as in wet, and to excuse them we shall have to dig deeper than the social system right down into the most ancient things-as-they-used-to-be. For an example which seems to come straight out of the most unpleasant fancies of the Marquis de Sade, we might contemplate the atrocious behavior of the so-called tarantula spider of the sandy wastes. Here, unfortunately, is a lover whom all the world will find it difficult to love.

This tarantula is a great hairy fellow much like the kind which sometimes comes north in a bunch of bananas and which most people have seen exhibited under a glass in some fruiterer's window. Most visitors to the desert hate and fear him at sight, even though he is disinclined to trouble human beings and is incapable even upon extreme provocation of giving more than a not-too-serious bite. Yet he does look more dangerous than the scorpion and he is, if possible, even less popular.

He has a leg spread of four or sometimes of as much as six inches, and it is said that he can leap for as much as two feet when pouncing upon his insect prey. Most of the time he spends in rather neat tunnels or burrows excavated in the sand, from which entomologists in search of specimens flush him out with water. And it is chiefly in the hottest months, especially after some rain, that one sees him prowling about, often crossing a road and sometimes waiting at a screen door to be let in. Except for man, his most serious enemy is the "tarantula hawk," a large black-bodied wasp with orange-red wings, who pounces upon his larger antagonist, paralyzes him with a sting and carries his now helpless body to feed the young wasps which will hatch in their own underground burrow.

Just to look at the tarantula's hairy legs and set of gleaming eyes is to suspect him of unconventionality or worse, and the suspicions are justified. He is one of those creatures in whom love seems to bring out the worst. Moreover, because at least one of the several species happens to have been the subject of careful study, the details are public. About the only thing he cannot be accused of is "infantile sexuality," and he can't be accused of that only because the male requires some eleven years to reach sexual maturity or even to develop the special organs necessary for his love making—if you can stretch this euphemistic term far enough to include his activities.

When at last he has come of age, he puts off the necessity of risking contact with a female as long as possible.

First he spins a sort of web into which he deposits a few drops of sperm. Then he patiently taps the web for a period of about two hours in order to fill with the sperm the two special palps or mouth parts which he did not acquire until the molt which announced his maturity. Then, and only then, does he go off in search of his "mystic and somber Dolores" who will never exhibit toward him any tender emotions.

If, as is often the case, she shows at first no awareness of his presence, he will give her a few slaps until she rears angrily with her fangs spread for a kill. At this moment he then plays a trick which nature, knowing the disposition of his mate, has taught him and for which nature has provided a special apparatus. He slips two spurs conveniently placed on his forelegs over the fangs of the female, in such a way that the fangs are locked into immobility. Then he transfers the sperm which he has been carrying into an orifice in the female, unlocks her fangs and darts away. If he is successful in making his escape, he may repeat the process with as many as three other females. But by this time he is plainly senile and he slowly dies, presumably satisfied that his life work has been accomplished. Somewhat unfairly, the female may live for a dozen more years and use up several husbands. In general outline the procedure is the same for many spiders, but it seems worse in him, because he is big enough to be conspicuous.

It is said that when indiscreet birdbanders announced their discovery that demure little house wrens commonly swap mates between the first and second of their summer broods, these wrens lost favor with many old ladies who promptly took down their nesting boxes because they refused to countenance such loose behavior.

In the case of the tarantula we have been contemplating mores which are far worse. But there ought, it seems to me, to be some possible attitude less unreasonable than either that of the old ladies who draw away from nature when she seems not to come up to their very exacting standards of behavior, and the seemingly opposite attitude of inverted romantics who are prone either to find all beasts other than man completely beastly, or to argue that since man is biologically a beast, nothing should or can be expected of him that is not found in all his fellow creatures.

Such a more reasonable attitude will, it seems to me, have to be founded on the realization that sex has had a history almost as long as the history of life, that its manifestations are as multifarious as the forms assumed by living things and that their comeliness varies as much as do the organisms themselves. Man did not invent it and he was not the first to exploit either the techniques of love making or the emotional and aesthetic themes which have become associated with them. Everything either beautiful or ugly of which he has found himself capable is somewhere anticipated in the repertory of plant and animal behavior. In some creatures sex seems a bare and mechanical necessity; in others the opportunity for elaboration has been seized upon and developed in many different directions. Far below the human level, love can be a game on the one hand, or a self-destructive passion on the other. It can inspire tenderness or cruelty; it can achieve fulfillment through either violent domination or prolonged solicitation. One is almost tempted to say that to primitive creatures, as to man, it can be sacred or profane, love or lust.

The tarantula's copulation is always violent rape and usually ends in death for the aggressor. But over against that may be set not only the romance of many birds but also of other less engaging creatures in whom nevertheless a romantic courtship is succeeded by an epoch of domestic attachment and parental solicitude. There is no justification for assuming, as some romanticists do, that the one is actually more "natural" than the other. In one sense nature is neither for nor against what have come to be human ideals. She includes both what we call good and what we call evil. We are simply among her experiments, though we are, in some respects, the most successful.

Some desert creatures have come quite a long way from the tarantula—and in our direction, too. Even those who have come only a relatively short way are already no longer repulsive. Watching from a blind two parent deer guarding a fawn while he took the first drink at a water hole, it seemed that the deer at least had come a long way.

To be sure many animals are, if this is possible, more "sex obsessed" than we—intermittently at least. Mating is the supreme moment of their lives and for many, as for the male scorpion and the male tarantula, it is also the beginning of the end. Animals will take more trouble and run more risks than men usually will, and if the Strindbergs are right when they insist that the woman still wants to consume her mate, the biological origin of that grisly impulse is rooted in times which are probably more ancient than the conquest of dry land.

Our currently best-publicized student of human sexual conduct has argued that some of what are called "perver-

sions" in the human being—homosexuality, for example—
should be regarded as merely "normal variations" because
something analogous is sometimes observed in the animal
kingdom. But if that argument is valid then nothing in
the textbooks of psychopathology is "abnormal." Once
nature had established the fact of maleness and female-
ness, she seems to have experimented with every possible
variation on the theme. By comparison, Dr. Kinsey's most
adventurous subjects were hopelessly handicapped by the
anatomical and physiological limitations of the human being.

In the animal kingdom, monogamy, polygamy, polyan-
dry and promiscuity are only trivial variations. Nature
makes hermaphrodites, as well as Tiresiases who are alter-
nately of one sex and then the other; also hordes of neu-
ters among the bees and the ants. She causes some males
to attach themselves permanently to their females and
teaches others how to accomplish impregnation without
ever touching them. Some embrace for hours; some, like
Onan, scatter their seed. Many males in many different or-
ders—like the seahorse and the ostrich, for example—brood
the eggs, while others will eat them, if they get a chance,
quite as blandly as many females will eat their mate,
once his business is done. Various male spiders wave vari-
ously decorated legs before the eyes of a prospective
spouse in the hope (often vain) that she will not mistake
them for a meal just happening by. But husband-eating is
no commoner than child-eating. Both should be classed as
mere "normal variants" in human behavior if nothing except a parallel in the animal kingdom is necessary to establish that status. To her children nature seems to have
said, "Copulate you must. But beyond that there is no rule.

Do it in whatever way and with whatever emotional concomitants you choose. That you should do it somehow or other is all that I ask."

If one confines one's attention too closely to these seamy sides, one begins to understand why, according to Gibbon, some early Fathers of the Church held that sex was the curse pronounced upon Adam and that, had he not sinned, the human race would have been propagated "by some harmless process of vegetation." Or perhaps one begins to repeat with serious emphasis the famous question once asked by the Messrs. Thurber and White, "Is Sex Necessary?" And the answer is that, strictly speaking, it isn't. Presumably the very first organisms were sexless. They reproduced by a "process of vegetation" so harmless that not even vegetable sexuality was involved. What is even more impressive is the patent fact that it is not necessary today. Some of the most successful of all plants and animals—if by successful you mean abundantly surviving—have given it up either entirely or almost entirely. A virgin birth may require a miracle if the virgin is to belong to the human race, but there is nothing miraculous about it in the case of many of nature's successful children. Parthenogenesis, as the biologist calls it, is a perfectly normal event.

Ask the average man for a serious answer to the question what sex is "for" or why it is "necessary," and he will probably answer without thinking that it is "necessary for reproduction." But the biologist knows that it is not. Actually the function of sex is not to assure reproduction but to prevent it—if you take the word literally and hence to mean "exact duplication." Both animals and plants could "reproduce" or "duplicate" without sex. But without it there would be little or no variation, heredities could not be mixed, unexpected combinations could not arise, and evolution would either never have taken place at all or, at least, taken place so slowly that we might all still be arthropods or worse.

If in both the plant and animal kingdom many organisms are actually abandoning the whole of the sexual process, that is apparently because they have resigned their interest in change and its possibilities. Everyone knows how the ants and the bees have increased the single-minded efficiency of the worker majority by depriving them of a sexual function and then creating a special class of sexual individuals. But their solution is far less radical than that of many of the small creatures, including many insects, some of whom are making sexless rather than sexual reproduction the rule, and some of whom are apparently dispensing with the sexual entirely so that no male has ever been found.

In the plant world one of the most familiar and successful of all weeds produces its seeds without pollinization, despite the fact that it still retains the flower which was developed long ago as a mechanism for facilitating that very sexual process which it has now given up. That it is highly "successful" by purely biological standards no one who has ever tried to eliminate dandelions from a lawn is likely to doubt. As I have said before, they not only get along very well in the world, they have also been astonishing colonizers here, since the white man unintentionally brought them from Europe, probably in hay. Sexless though the dandelion is, it is inheriting the earth, and the only penalty which it has to pay for its sexlessness is the penalty of abandoning all hope of ever being anything except a dandelion, even of being a better dandelion than it is. It seems to have said at some point, "This is good enough for me. My tribe flourishes. We have found how to get along in the world. Why risk anything?"

But if, from the strict biological standpoint, sex is "nothing but" a mechanism for encouraging variation, that is a long way from saying that there are not other standpoints. It is perfectly legitimate to say that it is also "for" many other things. Few other mechanisms ever invented or stumbled upon opened so many possibilities, entailed so many unforeseen consequences. Even in the face of those who refuse to entertain the possibility that any kind of purpose or foreknowledge guided evolution, we can still find it permissible to maintain that every invention is "for" whatever uses or good results may come from it, that all things, far from being "nothing but" their origins, are whatever they have become. Grant that and one must grant also that the writing of sonnets is one of the things which sex is "for."

Certainly nature herself discovered a very long time ago that sex was—or at least could be used—"for" many things besides the production of offspring not too monotonously like the parent. Certainly also, these discoveries anticipated pretty nearly everything which man himself has ever found it possible to use sex "for." In fact it becomes somewhat humiliating to realize that we seem to have invented nothing absolutely new.

Marital attachment? Attachment to the home? Devotion to children? Long before us, members of the animal kingdom had associated them all with sex. Before us they also founded social groups on the family unit and in some few cases even established monogamy as the rule! Even more strikingly, perhaps, many of them abandoned *force majeure* as the decisive factor in the formation of a mating pair and substituted for it courtships, which became a game, a ritual and an aesthetic experience. Every device of courtship known to the human being was exploited by his predecessors: colorful costume display, song, dance and the wafted perfume. And like man himself, certain animals have come to find the preliminary ceremonies so engaging that they prolong them far beyond the point where they have any justification outside themselves. The grasshopper, for instance, continues to sing like a troubadour long after the lady is weary with waiting.

Even more humiliating, perhaps, than the fact that we have invented nothing is the further fact that the evolution has not been in a straight line from the lowest animal families up to us. The mammals, who are our immediate ancestors, lost as well as gained in the course of their development. No doubt because they lost the power to see colors (which was not recaptured until the primates emerged), the appeal of the eye plays little part in their courtship. In fact "love" in most of its manifestations tends to play a much lesser part in their lives than in that of many lower creatures—even in some who are distinctly less gifted than the outstandingly emotional and aesthetic birds. On the whole, mammalian sex tends to be direct, unadorned, often brutal, and not even the apes, despite their recovery from color blindness, seem to have got very far beyond the most uncomplicated erotic experiences and practices. Intellectually the mammals may be closer to us than any other order of animals, but emotionally and aesthetically they are more remote than some others

—which perhaps explains the odd fact that most comparisons with any of them, and all comparisons with the primates, are derogatory. You may call a woman a "butterfly" or describe her as "birdlike." You may even call a man "leonine." But there is no likening with an ape which is not insulting.

How consciously, how poetically or how nobly each particular kind of creature may have learned to love, Venus only knows. But at this very moment of the desert spring many living creatures, plant as well as animal, are celebrating her rites in accordance with the tradition which happens to be theirs.

Fortunately, it is still too early for the tarantulas to have begun their amatory black mass, which, for all I know, may represent one of the oldest versions of the rituals still practiced in the worship of Mr. Swinburne's "mystic and somber Dolores." But this very evening as twilight falls, hundreds of moths will begin to stir themselves in the dusk and presently start their mysterious operations in the heart of those yucca blossoms which are just now beginning to open on the more precocious plants. Young jack rabbits not yet quite the size of an adult cottontail are proof that their parents went early about their business, and many of the brightly colored birds—orioles, cardinals and tanagers—are either constructing their nests or brooding their eggs. Some creatures seem to be worshiping only Venus Pandemos; some others have begun to have some inkling that the goddess manifests herself also as the atavist which the ancients called Venus Eurania. But it is patent to anyone who will take the trouble to look that they stand now upon different rungs of that Platonic ladder of love which man was certainly not the first to make some effort to climb.

Of this I am so sure that I feel it no betrayal of my humanity when I find myself entering with emotional sympathy into a spectacle which is more than a mere show, absorbing though it would be if it were no more than that. Modern knowledge gives me, I think, ample justification for the sense that I am not outside but a part of it, and if it did not give me that assurance, then I should probably agree that I would rather be "some pagan suckled in a creed outworn" than compelled to give it up.

Those very same biological sciences which have traced back to their lowly origins the emotional as well as the physiological characteristics of the sentient human being inevitably furnish grounds for the assumption that if we share much with the animals, they must at the same time share much with us. To maintain that all the conscious concomitants of our physical activities are without analogues in any creatures other than man is to fly in the face of the very evolutionary principles by which those "hardheaded" scientists set so much store. It is to assume that desire and joy have no origins in simpler forms of the same thing, that everything human has "evolved" except the consciousness which makes us aware of what we do. A Descartes, who held that man was an animal-machine differing from other animal-machines in that he alone possessed a gland into which God had inserted a soul, might consistently make between man and the other animals an absolute distinction. But the evolutionist is the last man who has a right to do anything of the sort.

He may, if he can consent to take the extreme position

of the pure behaviorist, maintain that in man and the animals alike consciousness neither is nor can be anything but a phosphorescent illusion on the surface of physiological action and reaction, and without any substantial reality or any real significance whatsoever. But there is no choice between that extreme position and recognition of the fact that animals, even perhaps animals as far down in the scale as any still living or preserved in the ancient rocks, were capable of some awareness and of something which was, potentially at least, an emotion.

Either love as well as sex is something which we share with animals, or it is something which does not really exist in us. Either it is legitimate to feel some involvement in the universal Rites of Spring, or it is not legitimate to take our own emotions seriously. And even if the choice between the two possibilities were no more than an arbitrary one, I know which of the alternatives I should choose to believe in and to live by.

T W E L V E

conservation is not enough

SUPPOSE THIS CHAPTER BEGAN BY SAYING THAT THE MORE thickly populated an area is, the fewer animals other than man will be found to be living there. No doubt I should be told not to waste my reader's time by telling him that. But the truth of the matter is that the statement would be false or questionable at best.

Consider for example a few square blocks in one of the most densely populated sections of New York City. There are, to be sure, probably fewer insects and worms below the surface of the soil than in the country. But if you count the rats, the mice, the cockroaches, the flies, the fleas, the bedbugs and the whatnots, the chances are that the nonhuman population above ground would be much greater than it is in most wild areas of equal extent. Even in the streets and in the air above there might well be more English sparrows than there are of all kinds of birds put together in a woodland-bordered meadow.

What we will have to say if we want to be truthful is something more like this: As man moves in, the larger, more conspicuous and, usually, the most attractive animals begin to disappear. Either they "take to the hills," go into hiding, or are exterminated in one way or another. What remain, and often prodigiously increase, are the creatures which either escape attention or find in the filth which crowds of men bring with them a rich pasture.

Even in a region as thinly populated by man as the Sonoran Desert, this law began long ago to operate. There are still a good many of the larger animals to be found if one looks for them in the right places. But they are both fewer and more wary than they were not so long ago. For them the problem of how to live in the desert was complicated by a new factor when man put in an appearance, and the technique which often becomes most completely indispensable reduces itself to one general principle: Keep out of his way. Moreover, the cover of darkness becomes more and more important and some, like the deer, which were once not nocturnal at all tend to become largely so. To find even the larger remaining animals the naturalist with the most benign intentions is compelled to act like a hunter and stalk his game.

A human community thus becomes a sort of sieve with the fineness of the mesh depending upon the thickness of the population. Just where I live, ten or twelve miles from Tucson, you might call the mesh "medium coarse." Jack rabbits as well as cottontails often come almost to my door and are pretty certain to spring up whenever one walks a few hundred yards toward the mountains. There are ground squirrel burrows all about, pack rats here and there and an occasional rock squirrel—a pepper-and-salt-colored creature about the size of an eastern gray squirrel but with a bushy tail which he always carries behind him instead of in orthodox squirrel fashion. Infrequently I hear at night the yipping of a coyote and on at least one occasion I have had to get porcupine quills out of the nose of a neighbor's dog. But all the larger, more spectacular mammals have been screened out, probably within the last decade. Double the distance from town and you may see deer crossing the road. Go twenty-five miles away to a forest ranger's cabin and the ring-tailed cats as well as the foxes sneak up for table scraps. There are even more sur-prising animals in the rugged area of recent volcanic mountains just west of town. But they have to be looked for.

Though I have never seen a mountain lion in the wild, they are quite common in some of the more mountain-ous regions of Arizona and one was shot not long ago thirty or forty miles away from here. Bobcats roam wild, if very wary, even closer at hand. A week or two ago I sat for a few hours in a photographer's blind beside a small man-made water hole about fifteen miles from town. First came a buck and a doe who stood on guard while their fawn took a long drink, then the curious little spotted skunk and, finally, two of the wild pigs or peccaries locally known as javelinas. At such a moment one feels that even

this close to a city there is some wilderness left. But if the
city continues to grow it will probably not be left much
longer. Deer and javelinas adapted themselves quite happily to the saguaro forest, nibbling the smaller cacti and
browsing on the fruit and leaves of desert shrubs. Mountain lions and bobcats kept the population within reasonable limits without exterminating it. But for the larger
mammals the question of how to live in the desert tends
to become unanswerable when the desert is inhabited by
man.

Some of us might be better reconciled to this fact if the
war to the death between man and the creatures whom
he is dispossessing really was necessary to man's own success. But much of the war is not and sometimes it actually
militates against him. To protect his sheep and cattle, the
rancher tries to destroy all the mountain lions and bobcats. He comes so near succeeding that the coyote population grows larger. He then enlists government aid to
poison the coyotes and when the coyotes are almost eliminated the ground squirrels and the gophers, on which the
coyotes fed, begin to get out of hand.

Somewhat belatedly, certain ranchers are beginning to
talk about protecting the coyote. If they ever get around
to it they will probably, in time, have to begin protecting
the mountain lion also. But by that time it probably will
be too late. If they had only been content to be a little
less thorough in the first place, we might all, including
the wild creatures, be better off. And a natural balance is
pleasanter than an artificial one, even when the artificial
can be made to work.

That this is no mere sentimentalist's fancy is attested by
the fact that at least one ranchers' association representing

more than 200,000 acres in Colorado has recently posted its land to forbid the killing of coyotes and taken as strong a stand on the whole matter. "We ranchers in the vicinity of Toponas, Colorado . . . are also opposed to the wide-spread destruction of weasels, hawks, eagles, skunks, foxes and other predatory animals. . . . The reason for this attitude is that for ten years or so we have watched the steady increase of mice, gophers, moles, rabbits and other rodents. Now we are at a point where these animals take up one-third of our hay crop. . . . What with government hunters and government poison . . . the coyote is nearly extinct in our part of the state. Foxes and bobcats have succumbed to the chain-killing poisons, etc. . . . This spring rodents have even killed sagebrush and quaking aspen trees . . . serious erosion is taking place."

Yet at last report the government was still setting cyanide gas guns and developing the "chain-poisoning" technique which involves killing animals with a poison that renders their carcasses deadly to the scavengers which eat them. And in Arizona the bounty on mountain lions continues.

Moralists often blame races and nations because they have never learned how to live and let live. In our time we seem to have been increasingly aware how persistently and brutally groups of men undertake to eliminate one another. But it is not only the members of his own kind that man seems to want to push off the earth. When he moves in, nearly everything else suffers from his intrusion —sometimes because he wants the space they occupy and the food they eat, but often simply because when he sees a creature not of his kind or a man not of his race his first impulse is "kill it."

Hence it is that even in the desert, where space is cheaper than in most places, the wild life grows scarcer and more secretive as the human population grows. The coyote howls further and further off. The deer seek closer and closer cover. To almost everything except man the smell of humanity is the most repulsive of all odors, the sight of man the most terrifying of all sights. Biologists call some animals "cryptozoic," that is to say "leading hidden lives." But as the human population increases most animals develop, as the deer has been developing, cryptozoic habits. Even now there are more of them around than we realize. They see us when we do not see them—because they have seen us first. Albert Schweitzer remarks somewhere that we owe kindness even to an insect when we can afford to show it, just because we ought to do something to make up for all the cruelties, necessary as well as unnecessary, which we have inflicted upon almost the whole of animate creation.

Probably not one man in ten is capable of understanding such moral and aesthetic considerations, much less of permitting his conduct to be guided by them. But perhaps twice as many, though still far from a majority, are beginning to realize that the reckless laying waste of the earth has practical consequences. They are at least beginning to hear about "conservation," though they are not even dimly aware of any connection between it and a large morality and are very unlikely to suppose that "conservation" does or could mean anything more than looking after their own welfare.

Hardly more than two generations ago Americans first

woke up to the fact that their land was not inexhaustible. Every year since then more and more has been said, and at least a little more has been done about "conserving resources," about "rational use" and about such reconstruction as seemed possible. Scientists have studied the problem, public works have been undertaken, laws passed. Yet everybody knows that the using up still goes on, perhaps not so fast nor so recklessly as once it did, but unmistakably nevertheless. And there is nowhere that it goes on more nakedly, more persistently or with a fuller realization of what is happening than in the desert regions where the margin to be used up is narrower.

First, more and more cattle were set to grazing and overgrazing the land from which the scanty rainfall now ran off even more rapidly than before. More outrageously still, large areas of desert shrub were rooted up to make way for cotton and other crops watered by wells tapping underground pools of water which are demonstrably shrinking fast. These pools represent years of accumulation not now being replenished and are exhaustible exactly as an oil well is exhaustible. Everyone knows that they will give out before long, very soon, in fact, if the number of wells continues to increase as it has been increasing. Soon dust bowls will be where was once a sparse but healthy desert, and man, having uprooted, slaughtered or driven away everything which lived healthily and normally there, will himself either abandon the country or die. There are places where the creosote bush is a more useful plant than cotton.

To the question why men will do or are permitted to do such things there are many answers. Some speak of population pressures, some more brutally of unconquerable human greed. Some despair; some hope that more education and more public works will, in the long run, prove effective. But is there, perhaps, something more, something different, which is indispensable? Is there some missing link in the chain of education, law and public works? Is there not something lacking without which none of these is sufficient?

After a lifetime spent in forestry, wild-life management and conservation of one kind or another, after such a lifetime during which he nevertheless saw his country slip two steps backward for every one it took forward, the late Aldo Leopold pondered the question and came up with an unusual answer which many people would dismiss as "sentimental" and be surprised to hear from a "practical" scientific man. He published his article originally in the *Journal of Forestry* and it was reprinted in the posthumous volume, *A Sand County Almanac,* where it was given the seemingly neutral but actually very significant title "The Land Ethic."

This is a subtle and original essay full of ideas never so clearly expressed before and seminal in the sense that each might easily grow into a separate treatise. Yet the conclusion reached can be simply stated. Something *is* lacking and because of that lack education, law and public works fail to accomplish what they hope to accomplish. Without that something, the high-minded impulse to educate, to legislate and to manage become as sounding brass and tinkling cymbals. And the thing which is missing is love, some feeling for, as well as some understanding of, the inclusive community of rocks and soils, plants and animals, of which we are a part.

It is not, to put Mr. Leopold's thoughts in different

words, enough to be enlightenedly selfish in our dealings with the land. That means, of course, that it is not enough for the farmer to want to get the most out of his farm and the lumberer to get the most out of his forest without considering agriculture and wood production as a whole both now and in the future. But it also means more than that. In the first place enlightened selfishness cannot be enough because enlightened selfishness cannot possibly be extended to include remote posterity. It may include the children, perhaps, and grandchildren, possibly, but it cannot be extended much beyond that because the very idea of "self" cannot be stretched much further. Some purely ethical considerations must operate, if anything does. Yet even that is not all. The wisest, the most enlightened, the most remotely long-seeing exploitation of resources is not enough, for the simple reason that the whole concept of exploitation is so false and so limited that in the end it will defeat itself and the earth will have been plundered no matter how scientifically and farseeingly the plundering has been done.

To live healthily and successfully on the land we must also live with it. We must be part not only of the human community, but of the whole community; we must acknowledge some sort of oneness not only with our neighbors, our countrymen and our civilization but also some respect for the natural as well as for the man-made community. Ours is not only "one world " in the sense usually implied by that term. It is also "one earth." Without some acknowledgment of that fact, men can no more live successfully than they can if they refuse to admit the political and economic interdependency of the various sections of the civilized world. It is not a sentimental but a grimly literal fact that unless we share this terrestrial globe with creatures other than ourselves, we shall not be able to live on it for long.

You may, if you like, think of this as a moral law. But if you are skeptical about moral laws, you cannot escape the fact that it has its factual, scientific aspect. Every day the science of ecology is making clearer the factual aspect as it demonstrates those more and more remote interdependencies which, no matter how remote they are, are crucial even for us.

Before even the most obvious aspects of the balance of nature had been recognized, a greedy, self-centered mankind naïvely divided plants into the useful and the useless. In the same way it divided animals into those which were either domestic on the one hand or "game" on the other, and the "vermin" which ought to be destroyed. That was the day when extermination of whole species was taken as a matter of course and random introductions which usually proved to be either complete failures or all too successful were everywhere being made. Soon, however, it became evident enough that to rid the world of vermin and to stock it with nothing but useful organisms was at least not a simple task—if you assume that "useful" means simply "immediately useful to man."

Yet even to this day the *ideal* remains the same for most people. They may know, or at least they may have been told, that what looks like the useless is often remotely but demonstrably essential. Out in this desert country they may see the land being rendered useless by overuse. They may even have heard how, when the mountain lion is killed off, the deer multiply; how, when the deer multiply, the new growth of trees and shrubs is eaten away;

and how, when the hills are denuded, a farm or a section of grazing land many miles away is washed into gulleys and made incapable of supporting either man or any other of the large animals. They may even have heard how the wonderful new insecticides proved so effective that fish and birds died of starvation; how on at least one Pacific island insects had to be reintroduced to pollinate the crops; how when you kill off almost completely a destructive pest, you run the risk of starving out everything which preys upon it and thus run the risk that the pest itself will stage an overwhelming comeback because its natural enemies are no more. Yet, knowing all this and much more, their dream is still the dream that an earth for man's use only can be created if only we learn more and scheme more effectively. They still hope that nature's scheme of checks and balances which provides for a varied population, which stubbornly refuses to scheme only from man's point of view and cherishes the weeds and "vermin" as persistently as she cherishes him, can be replaced by a scheme of his own devising. Ultimately they hope they can beat the game. But the more the ecologist learns, the less likely it seems that man can in the long run do anything of the sort.

"Nature's social union" is by no means the purely gentle thing which Burns imagined. In fact it is a balance, with all the stress and conflict which the word implies. In this sense it is not a "social union" at all. But it is, nevertheless, a workable, seesawing balance. And when it ceases to seesaw, there is trouble ahead for whatever is on the end that stays up, as well as for those on the end which went down

Thus, for every creature there is a paradox at the heart of the necessary "struggle for existence" and the paradox is simply this: Neither man nor any other animal can afford to triumph in that struggle too completely. Unconditional surrender is a self-defeating formula—even in the war against insect pests. To the victor belong the spoils in nature also, but for a time only. When there are no more spoils to be consumed, the victor dies. That is believed by some to be what happened to the dominant carnivorous dinosaurs many millions of years ago. They became too dominant and presently there was nothing left to dominate—or to eat. It is certainly what happens to other creatures like the too-protected deer in a national forest who multiply so successfully that their herds can no longer be fed, or, more spectacularly, like the lemmings who head desperately toward a new area to be exploited and end in the cold waters of the North Sea because that area does not exist.

Curiously, the too tender-minded dreamed a dream more attractive than that of the ruthless exploiters but no less unrealizable. They dreamed of "refuges" and "sanctuaries" where the "innocent" creatures might live in a perpetually peaceful paradise untroubled by such "evil" creatures as the fox and the hawk. But it required few experiments with such utopias to demonstrate that they will not work. A partridge covey or a deer herd which is not thinned by predators soon eats itself into starvation and suffers also from less obvious maladjustments. The overaged and the weaklings, who would have fallen first victims to their carnivorous enemies, survive to weaken the stock, and as overpopulation increases, the whole community becomes affected by some sort of nervous tension

—"shock" the ecologists call it—analogous to that which afflicts human beings crowded into congested areas.

No more striking evidence of this fact can be found than what happened when it was decided to "protect" the deer on the Kaibab Plateau in the Grand Canyon region. At the beginning of this century there was a population of about 4000 occupying some 127,000 acres. Over a period of years the mountain lions, wolves and coyotes which lived at its expense were pretty well exterminated. By 1924 the 4000 had become 100,000 and then calamity struck. In one year, 1924, 60,000 victims of starvation and disease disappeared and then, year by year, though at a decreasing rate, the population dwindled.

Wild creatures need their enemies as well as their friends. The red tooth and red claw are not the whole story but they are part of it, and the park superintendent with his gun "scientifically" redressing the balance is a poor but necessary substitute for the balance which the ages have established. We may find nature's plan cruel but we cannot get away from it entirely. The lion and the lamb will not—they simply cannot—lie down together, but they are essential to one another nonetheless. And the lesson to be learned is applicable far outside the field of conservation. It is that though the laws of nature may be mitigated, though their mitigation constitutes civilization, they cannot be abolished altogether.

So far as the problem is only that of the Kaibab deer, one common solution is the "open season" when man himself is encouraged to turn predator and hunters are permitted, as some conservationists put it, to "harvest the crop." To some this seems a repellent procedure and even

as a practical solution it is far from ideal. Other beasts of
prey destroy first the senile and the weaklings; man, if he
selects at all, selects the mature and the vigorous for
slaughter. The objection to this method is much the same
as it would be to a proposal that we should attack the
problem of human population by declaring an annual
open season on all between the ages of eighteen and
thirty-five. That is, of course, precisely what we do when
a war is declared, and there are those who believe that the
ultimate cause of wars is actually, though we are not
aware of the fact, the overgrazing of our own range and
the competition for what remains.

What is commonly called "conservation" will not work
in the long run because it is not really conservation at all
but rather, disguised by its elaborate scheming, only a
more knowledgeable variation of the old idea of a world
for man's use only. That idea is unrealizable. But how
can man be persuaded to cherish any other ideal unless he
can learn to take some interest and some delight in the
beauty and variety of the world for its own sake, unless he
can see a "value" in a flower blooming or an animal at
play, unless he can see some "use" in things not useful?

In our society we pride ourselves upon having reached
a point where we condemn an individual whose whole
aim in life is to acquire material wealth for himself. But
his vulgarity is only one step removed from that of a society which takes no thought for anything except increasing the material wealth of the community itself. In his
usual extravagant way Thoreau once said: "This curious

world which we inhabit is more wonderful than it is convenient; more beautiful than it is useful; it is more to be admired than it is to be used." Perhaps that "more" is beyond what most people could or perhaps ought to be convinced of. But without some realization that "this curious world" is at least beautiful as well as useful, "conservation" is doomed. We must live for something besides making a living. If we do not permit the earth to produce beauty and joy, it will in the end not produce food either.

Here practical considerations and those which are commonly called "moral," "aesthetic" and even "sentimental" join hands. Yet even the enlightened Department of Agriculture is so far from being fully enlightened that it encourages the farmer to forget that his land can ever produce anything except crops and is fanatical to the point of advising him how to build fences so that a field may be plowed to the last inch without leaving even that narrow margin in which one of the wild flowers—many of which agriculture has nearly rendered extinct—may continue to remind him that the world is beautiful as well as useful. And that brings us around to another of Aldo Leopold's seminal ideas:

> *Conservation still proceeds at a snail's pace; . . .*
> *the usual answer . . . is 'more conservation.' . . .*
> *But is it certain that only the* volume *of education*
> *needs stepping up? Is something lacking in* content *as*
> *well? . . . It is inconceivable to me that an ethical*
> *relation to land can exist without love, respect and*
> *admiration for land, and a high regard for its value.*
> *By value, I of course mean something far broader*
> *than mere economic value; I mean value in the phi-*
> *losophical sense.*

Here in the West, as in the country at large, a war more
or less concealed under the guise of a "conflict of interests"
rages between the "practical" conservationist and the de-
fenders of national parks and other public lands; between
cattlemen and lumberers on the one hand, and "sentimen-
talists" on the other. The pressure to allow the hunter,
the rancher or the woodcutter to invade the public domain
is constant and the plea is always that we should "use"
what is assumed to be useless unless it is adding to material welfare. But unless somebody teaches love, there can
be no ultimate protection to what is lusted after. Without
some "love of nature" for itself there is no possibility of
solving "the problem of conservation."

Any fully matured science of ecology will have to grap-
ple with the fact that from the ecological point of view,
man is one of those animals which is in danger from its
too successful participation in the struggle for existence.
He has upset the balance of nature to a point where
he has exterminated hundreds of other animals and ex-
hausted soils. Part of this he calls a demonstration of his
intelligence and of the success which results from his use
of it. But because of that intelligence he has learned how
to exploit resources very thoroughly and he is even beginning to learn how to redress the balance in certain minor
ways. But he cannot keep indefinitely just one step ahead
of overcrowding and starvation. From the standpoint of
nature as a whole, he is both a threat to every other living
thing and, therefore, a threat to himself also. If he were
not so extravagantly successful it would be better for
nearly everything except man and, possibly therefore, better, in the longest run, for him also. He has become the
tyrant of the earth, the waster of its resources, the creator

of the most prodigious imbalance in the natural order which has ever existed.

From a purely homocentric point of view this may seem entirely proper. To most people it undoubtedly does. Is it not our proudest boast that we have learned how to "control nature"? Does not our dream of the future include a final emancipation from any dependence upon a natural balance and the substitution for it of some balance established by ourselves and in our exclusive interest? Is not that, in fact, what most people have in mind when they think of the final triumph of humanity?

But what every "practical" ecologist is trying to do is maintain the balance of nature without facing the fact that man himself is part of it, that you cannot hope to keep the balance unless you admit that to some extent the immediate interest of the human species may sometimes have to be disregarded. No other single fact is so important as man himself in creating the often disastrous imbalances which continually develop. It is not possible to re-establish them for long without undertaking to control the organism which has most obviously entered upon a runaway phase. Must we not recognize the fact that any real "management of resources" is impossible unless we are willing to sacrifice to some extent the immediate interests not only of certain individual men but also those of the human species itself? Most of us have reached the point where we recognize that the immediate interests of the lumberman or the rancher must sometimes be sacrificed to "the general good." Ultimately we may have to recognize that there is also a conflict between what is called the general good and a good still more general—the good, that is to say, of the whole biological community.

The more completely we bring nature "under control," the more complicated our methods must become, the more disastrous the chain reaction which is set up by any failure of wisdom, or watchfulness, or technique. We are required to know more and more and we are always threatened by the impossibility of achieving adequate knowledge, much less of adequate wisdom and virtue.

Every increase in the complexity of organization has made the situation more precarious at the same time that it has increased our comfort and our wealth. Until we learned to support a population far larger than would have been believed possible a century ago, there was no danger of general starvation, however disastrous and common local famines may have been, and though Malthus was obviously wrong in his estimates, it is by no means certain that he was wrong in his general principle. Until we increased the wealth of nations by linking them one with another we were not exposed to the danger of world-wide economic collapse. Until we learned how to "control" the atom there was no danger that atomic phenomena would get out of control and hence it is still not clear whether we are running machines or machines are running us. We have three tigers—the economic, the physical and the biological—by the tail and three tigers are more than three times as dangerous as one. We cannot let any of them go. But it is also not certain that we can hold all of them indefinitely. Many a despot has discovered that it was just when his power seemed to have been made absolute at last that the revolution broke out. And it may be that just about three hundred years was necessary to expose the fallacy of the ideal born in the seventeenth century.

If one is prepared to admit that there is a limit to the

extent to which we can exercise a biological control exclusively in our own interest, then it is certainly worthwhile to ask how we might know when we are approaching that limit.

It will hardly do to say simply that the limit has been passed when a society is obviously sick. Too many different reasons have been given to explain that sickness, and several of them can be made to seem more or less convincing—indeed, several of them may be partially correct. But there is a criterion which it seems to me not wholly fanciful to apply.

Might it not have something to do with nature's own great principle, live and let live? Might it not be that man's success as an organism is genuinely a success so long, but only so long, as it does not threaten the extinction of everything not useful to and absolutely controlled by him; so long as that success is not incompatible with the success of nature as the varied and free thing which she is; so long as, to some extent, man is prepared to share the earth with others?

If by any chance that criterion is valid, then either one of two things is likely to happen. Perhaps outraged nature will violently reassert herself and some catastrophe, perhaps the catastrophe brought about when more men are trying to live in our limited space than even their most advanced technology can make possible, will demonstrate the hollowness of his supposed success. Perhaps, on the other hand, man himself will learn in time to set a reasonable limit to his ambitions and accept the necessity of recognizing his position as the most highly evolved of living creatures but not, therefore, entitled to assume that no others have a right to live unless they contribute directly to his material welfare.

The now popular saying, "No man is an island," means more than it is commonly taken to mean. Not only men but all living things stand or fall together. Or rather man is of all such creatures one of those least able to stand alone. If we think only in terms of our own welfare we are likely to find that we are losing it.

But how can man learn to accept such a situation, to believe that it is right and proper when the whole tendency of his thought and his interest carries him in a contrary direction? How can he learn to value and delight in a natural order larger than his own order? How can he come to accept, not sullenly but gladly, the necessity of sharing the earth?

As long ago as the seventeenth century, as long ago, that is, as the very time when the ambition to "control nature" in any large ambitious way was first coming to be formulated and embraced, a sort of answer to these questions was being given in theological terms. John Ray, one of the first great English biologists, formulated them in a book which was read for a hundred years, and what Ray had to say cuts two ways because it was directed against the egotism of man as expressed both by the old-fashioned theologians who thought that everything had been *made* for man's use and by the Baconians who assumed that he could at least *turn it* to that use.

"It is," Ray wrote, "a general received opinion, that all this visible world was created for Man; that Man is the

End of Creation; as if there were no other end of any creature, but some way or other to be serviceable to man. . . . But though this be vulgarly received, yet wise men now-a-days think otherwise. Dr. Moore affirms, that creatures are made to enjoy themselves as well as to serve us." The greatest profit which we can get from the observation and study of other living things is, Ray went on to say, often not that we learn how to use them but that we may contemplate through them the wonders and the beauties of God's creation. What Ray was saying is precisely what Thoreau was restating in secularized form when he insisted that "this curious world which we inhabit . . . is more to be admired and enjoyed than it is to be used."

Since our age is not inclined to be interested in theological arguments, it is not likely to find Ray's exposition a sufficient reason for accepting gladly the continued existence on this earth of "useless" plants and animals occupying space which man might turn to his own immediate profit. Our generation is more likely to make at least certain concessions in that direction as the result of absorbing what the ecologist has to say about the impossibility of maintaining a workable balance without a much more generous view of what is "useful" and what is not. But it is not certain that on that basis man will ever make quite enough concessions and it *is* entirely certain that he will not make them happily, will not find life pleasanter just because he makes them, unless he can learn to love and to delight in the variety of nature.

Perhaps, if we cannot send him as far back as the seventeenth century to be taught, we can at least send him back to the eighteenth. Pope, speaking half for metaphysics and half for science, could write:

Has God, thou fool! worked solely for thy good,
Thy joy, thy pastime, thy attire, thy food?
        .   .   .   .

Know, Nature's children all divide her care;
The fur that warms a monarch, warmed a bear.

This is precisely what most men even two centuries later
do not really understand.

THIRTEEN

the mystique of the desert

TO MOST LAYMEN AS WELL AS TO MANY PROFESSIONALS
the word "science" means "a collection of observable facts
about the physical universe." And there are many who
profess to believe that beyond such observable facts we
should never allow our minds to wander.

Actually, however, no one ever did stop there. No human being is so completely unspeculative, so totally devoid
of imagination, so incapable of drawing general conclu-
sions, that he does not go on from observable facts to draw
morals, to set up standards of value and to philosophize in

one way or another. He does so even at the very moment when he is assuring himself that he will do nothing of the sort. Even to say that one has no philosophy is to have one.

More than two thousand years ago Aristotle coined the word "metaphysics"—which means "beyond physics"—in order to give a name to that whole realm of intellectual activity which begins where the observation and organization of physical facts leaves off. More recently, Bernard Shaw, half-jokingly perhaps, has coined on the same model another word, "metabiology." Time has not tested it so thoroughly as it has tested Aristotle's "metaphysics" but it may turn out to be useful by calling attention to an important fact.

Both words suggest that such subjects of inquiry as morals (or the nature of the good) and aesthetics (or the nature of the beautiful) lie beyond the reach of that kind of positive knowledge with which the physical sciences deal. But there is a difference between what Aristotle's word seems to imply and what Shaw's word is intended to suggest. Meta*physics* seems to accept the recent assumption that life itself is reducible to physical and chemical laws and to imply, therefore, that moral and aesthetic questions can best be answered by referring them to the laws of the physical universe. Meta*biology*, on the other hand, suggests that since life itself is not completely explainable in merely physical terms, moral and aesthetic questions should be discussed in connection with what we know about living creatures without any attempt to reduce such questions to merely physical terms. The difference, in other words, is the difference between the purely materialistic, mechanistic approach to such questions, which is favored by the so-called "positivists," and an approach which recognizes that living things, being radically different from inanimate objects, are capable of standards of value which correspond to nothing in the merely physical world.

If your ethics, your aesthetics, your epistomology even, are things which lie immediately beyond what you know or think you know about the phenomena associated with living creatures; if these seem to you a better taking-off place than facts about mechanics or even chemistry, then your metaphysical convictions will take on a color sufficiently distinctive to justify a distinctive name. And if you attempt, as Shaw did, to formulate these convictions into a consistent system, then you may quite properly call yourself not so much a "metaphysician" as a "metabiologist."

Shaw was, of course, thinking especially of what seemed to him to follow from his own belief that evolution is the most important of all observable facts and that what evolution reveals is not merely a Darwinian mechanism but the effectiveness, throughout all time, of the imagination which can dream of something better and the will which can make the dream come true. Upon that conviction he based his philosophy, his metaphysics, or, as he preferred to call it, his metabiology.

Whether one accepts Shaw's conviction or not—and most biologists will, I imagine, shake their heads—the fact remains that a great many of us are today "metabiologists" of one sort or another whether we realize it or not. And by that I mean simply that for us the most important of all the "collections of observable facts" which the centuries have accumulated are those which concern the behavior of living creatures. And it is "beyond" these facts that, for us, the most significant philosophy must lie.

People nowadays are less interested in theology than they were in times gone by. They are not interested because they do not believe that they have any facts about God upon which, or just beyond which, metaphysical convictions about Him could be based. Perhaps most people are, whether they know it or not, simple positivists in the sense that they believe that even man is a machine wholly explainable in physical terms. But there is an increasing number who feel that the attempt to account for life in purely physical terms has failed. They may continue to insist that no available evidence suggests the existence of any God. But they also insist that life is not demonstrably "merely chemical" and that biology must recognize realities not either physical or chemical.

For them, therefore, philosophy lies "beyond" biology, not beyond physics. For them the place to start that philosophy is not with physics or with chemistry but with life itself as a fact no less primary than the facts of physics and chemistry. Because I myself make that assumption, many of the speculations in which I have permitted myself to indulge in this book are heretical from the conventional biologist's point of view. But the heresy seems to me to have a desirable consequence—it redeems the universe from that deadness which mechanistic science has increasingly attributed to it.

Let us suppose that you are "interested in nature"—at least to the extent that anyone who has willingly read thus far in this book must be. If that means only that it somehow pleases you to know that road runners eat snakes, that Gila monsters are our sole poisonous lizards, or that the cacti are native to the New World only, then your interest is "scientific" in the most limited possible sense of the term. If you go beyond that to the extent of trying to learn how this scientific knowledge may be useful to man in his struggle to feed himself well or to preserve his health, then your interest is both scientific in the limited sense and also "technological." But as soon as you take the next step and begin to ask yourself not merely what immediate practical use can be made of known facts but also what they suggest to the speculative mind about the potentialities and limitations of living matter; as soon as you begin to find yourself thinking of what the human mind cannot help calling the "intentions" and "the standards of value" which nature pursues, then you have entered the realm of the metabiological.

Any consideration of evolution, for instance, becomes metabiological as soon as it abandons a mere description of the evolutionary process to permit itself to refer even cautiously to "higher" and "lower" forms of life, to celebrate "growth" and "change" and "survival value" as moral concepts; at that point the consideration has gone "beyond" the narrow limits of the science of biology and become metaphysical, or metabiological, no matter what you may prefer to call it. Similarly, ecology is narrowly scientific when it merely describes the interrelations of living things. It is narrowly technological when it seeks to learn only how forests can be preserved and farms kept fertile through the application of our knowledge. And so long as it is interested in nothing except "land management," for instance, it remains just technological and nothing more. But when it begins to develop what Aldo Leopold called a "land ethic," then it is "beyond" either science or technology because any sort of ethic is metaphysical and an ethic erected upon our knowledge of biology is specifically "metabiological."

I hope that when in this book I have described some aspect of desert life it has usually been clear that the metabiology of the desert is one of the things which has interested me most. If it had not interested me, I do not think that I would ever have concerned myself much with either science or technology. Moreover, having said that—and I realize that to say even so much is to condemn myself in the eyes of a certain class of scientist and technician—I must confess to something even worse. I must confess that there are moments when what seems most important of all is something of which the metabiologist may be almost as suspicious as the strict biologist is suspicious of the metabiological.

Just as the realm of speculative reason lies beyond the facts of science, so also, beyond the realm of speculative reason, lies the realm of emotion. To me that realm is no less important than the realm of fact or the realm of speculative thought, though to discuss what one experiences in the realm of emotion one must either depreciate it and explain it away, as the pure rationalist does, or one must accept what one can only call the *mystique* as opposed to the *rational* of the human being's intercourse with the universe around him.

Your Philistine never enters this realm of the mystical. When he has read the great poem, looked at the great picture, heard the great music, or even grasped the great theory, he always makes the same comments in words which lie halfway between exclamation and question: "So what?" Since neither music, nor poetry, nor pure theory has practical usefulness, and since the mystique of all three eludes him, his comment-question is perfectly proper. And the only—usually impossible—answer to him lies in the mystique itself.

Though in this book I have presented facts and, at moments, permitted myself metabiological speculations, neither the one nor the other really says all that I would like to be able to say. If Dipodomys never drinks; if the moth desires the candle; if the seed has learned to disregard the wetness of summer while waiting for the wetness of spring; if the cactus has learned to be at home where its ancestors would have perished; who cares? Why, having learned these things, did I not say, "So what" and pass on? The ultimate answer, I think, is to be found only by admitting the mystical element. The reason for my deepest caring does not lie within the scope of biology or even metabiology. One cannot recognize it without being to that extent a mystic.

Of the official mystical writers I am no great reader. The clarity of their visions, the overwhelming certainty of their conviction that ultimate truth has been revealed to them, is foreign to my own experience. At most I have "intimations," not assurances, and I doubt that I could ever go further in recommendation of the complete mystics than William James goes when he bids the ordinary mortal recognize the reality, in some realm, of the phenomena to which the mystics testify, no matter what interpretation we ordinary mortals put upon them. Yet I, and many whose temperaments are no more mystical than mine, do know moments when we draw courage and joy from experiences which lie outside the getting and spending of everyday life.

The occasions of such experiences are many. The commonest and perhaps the least obviously related are these: reading a poem and contemplating a child—human or animal. But the experiences come to different men in many different ways. Some are most likely to be aware of them in solitude, others in crowds; some while looking at the stars, some while watching the waves roll in upon a beach. And whether you call the experience infrarational or superrational, it involves the momentary acceptance of values not definable in terms of that common sense to which we ordinarily accord our first loyalty. And to all such experiences one thing is common. There is a sense of satisfaction which is not personal but impersonal. One no longer asks, "What's in it for me?" because one is no longer a separate selfish individual but part of the welfare and joy of the whole.

Those to whom such mystical experiences are habitual and hence more ordinary than what most people call ordinary life, can often call upon them at will as the religious mystics do by the repetition of a prayer. But to the majority there is no certain formula or ritual—not even a private, much less a communicable, one. At most we can only, for example, plunge into the crowd or retire into a solitude, knowing that sometimes in the one situation or the other we will glimpse out of the corner of our eyes what, if one may believe the true mystics, is usually at the very center of the true mystic's vision.

I happen to be one of those, and we are not a few, to whom the acute awareness of a natural phenomenon, especially of a phenomenon of the living world, is the thing most likely to open the door to that joy we cannot analyze. I have experienced it sometimes when a rabbit appeared suddenly from a bush to dash away to the safety which he values so much, or when, at night, a rustle in the leaves reminds me how many busy lives surround my own. It has also come almost as vividly when I suddenly saw a flower opening or a stem pushing out of the ground.

But what is the content of the experience? What is it that at such moments I seem to realize? Of what is my happiness compounded?

First of all, perhaps, there is the vivid assurance that these things, that the universe itself, really do exist, that life is not a dream; second, that the reality is pervasive and, it seems, unconquerable. The future of mankind is dubious. Perhaps the future of the whole earth is only somewhat less dubious. But one knows that all does not depend upon man, that possibly, even, it does not depend upon this earth. Should man disappear, rabbits may well still run and flowers may still open. If this globe itself should perish, then it seems not unreasonable to suppose that what inspires the stem and the flower may exist somewhere else. And I, it seems, am at least part of all this.

God looked upon the world and found that it was good. How great is the happiness of being able, even for a moment, to agree with Him! And how much easier that is if one is not committed to considering only some one section of the world or of the universe.

Long before I ever saw the desert I was aware of the mystical overtones which the observation of nature made audible to me. But I have never been more frequently or more vividly aware of them than in connection with the desert phenomena. And I have often wondered why.

Were I to believe what certain psychologists have been trying to tell me, the thing which I call a "mystique" and especially what I call "the mystique of the desert" is only the vague aura left behind by certain experiences of infancy and childhood. Should I search my memory of the latter I should certainly find there what nearly every other American or European would: a Christmas card showing Wise Men crossing the desert and also, in some school geography, another picture of rolling dunes, a camel and the caption, "Sahara Desert." Both seemed then to be things I should never see; both were remote from the scene of my sorrows—whatever at the moment I found my sorrows to be. "Poof!" say those psychologists. The "mystique" is mysterious no longer. To adjust yourself to your environment would have been a simple matter. Had you been so adjusted you would never have gone to live in the American Southwest. And you would not give a damn whether Dipodomys drinks or not.

If those psychologists are right, then I am glad that I, at least, was not "adjusted" to everything and hence incapable of giving a damn about anything whatsoever. But I am not sure that they *are* right. Curiosity is not always the result of conditioning and there are words at which most imaginations kindle. Among them are all those words which suggest the untamed extravagances or the ultimate limits of nature in any one of her moods. We may prefer to live amid hills and meadows, fields and woodlots, or even, for that matter, surrounded by steel and concrete. But "wilderness," "jungle," and "desert" are still stirring words, as even movie-makers know. And it is just possible that they will continue to be such after the last Christmas card having anything to do with Christmas has disappeared from the shops and after school geographies have consented to confine themselves exclusively to "things relevant to the child's daily life." Perhaps the mind is not merely a blank slate upon which anything may be written. Perhaps it reaches out spontaneously toward what can nourish either intelligence or imagination. Perhaps it is part of nature and, without being taught, shares nature's intentions.

Most of the phrases we use glibly to exorcise or explain away the realities of our intimate experience are of quite recent origin—phrases like "emotional conditioning," "complex," "fixation," and even "reflex." But one of the most inclusive, and the most relevant here, is older. It was Ruskin, of all people, who invented the term "pathetic fallacy" to stigmatize as in some sense unjustified our tendency to perceive a smiling landscape as "happy," a somber one as "sad." But is it really a fallacy? Are we so separate from nature that our states are actually discontinuous with it? Is there nothing outside ourselves which is somehow glad or sad? Is it really a fallacy when we attribute to nature feelings analogous to our own?

Out of the very heart of the romantic feeling for nature the question arose. And it was Coleridge, again of all people, who gave the answer upon which the post-romantic "scientific" attitude rests: "Only in ourselves does nature live." But Wordsworth, who recorded Coleridge's dictum, was not himself always sure. When he was most himself it seemed to him that, on the contrary, the joy of nature was older than the joy of man and that what was transitory in the individual was permanent somewhere else. When the moment of happiness passed, it was not because the glory had faded but only because his own sight had grown dim.

There was a time when meadow, grove, and stream,
The earth, and every common sight,
        To me did seem
Apparelled in celestial light,
The glory and the freshness of a dream.

Oh joy! that in our embers
Is something that doth live,
That nature yet remembers
What was so fugitive!

Something like this is what, in clumsy prose, I am try-ing to suggest. "Wilderness," "jungle," "desert," are not magic words because we have been "conditioned" to find them such but because they stand for things which only conditioning can make seem indifferent or alien. How could the part be greater than the whole? How can na-ture's meaning come wholly from man when he is only part of that meaning? "Only in ourselves does nature live" is less true than its opposite: "Only in nature do *we* have a being."

The most materialistic of historians do not deny the in-fluence upon a people of the land on which they live. When they say, for instance, that the existence of a frontier was a dominant factor in shaping the character of the American people, they are not thinking only of a physical fact. They mean also that the idea of a frontier, the reali-zation that space to be occupied lay beyond it, took its place in the American imagination and sparked the sense that there was "somewhere else to go" rather than that the solution of every problem, practical or spiritual, had to be found within the limits to which the man who faced them was confined.

In the history of many other peoples the character of their land, even the very look of the landscape itself, has powerfully influenced how they felt and what they thought about. They were woodsmen or plainsmen or mountaineers not only economically but spiritually also. And nothing, not even the sea, has seemed to affect men more profoundly than the desert, or seemed to incline them so powerfully toward great thoughts, perhaps because the desert itself seems to brood and to encourage brooding. To the Hebrews the desert spoke of God, and one of the most powerful of all religions was born. To the Arabs it spoke of the stars, and astronomy came into being.

Perhaps no fact about the American people is more important than the fact that the continent upon which they live is large enough and varied enough to speak with many different voices—of the mountains, of the plains, of the valleys and of the seashore—all clear voices that are distinct and strong. Because Americans listened to all these voices, the national character has had many aspects and developed in many different directions. But the voice of the desert is the one which has been least often heard. We came to it last, and when we did come, we came principally to exploit rather than to listen.

To those who do listen, the desert speaks of things with an emphasis quite different from that of the shore, the mountains, the valleys or the plains. Whereas they invite action and suggest limitless opportunity, exhaustless resources, the implications and the mood of the desert are something different. For one thing the desert is conservative, not radical. It is more likely to provoke awe than to invite conquest. It does not, like the plains, say, "Only turn the sod and uncountable riches will spring up." The heroism which it encourages is the heroism of endurance, not that of conquest.

Precisely what other things it says depends in part upon the person listening. To the biologist it speaks first of the remarkable flexibility of living things, of the processes of adaptation which are nowhere more remarkable than in the strange devices by which plants and animals have learned to conquer heat and dryness. To the practical-minded conservationist it speaks sternly of other things, because in the desert the problems created by erosion and overexploitation are plainer and more acute than anywhere else. But to the merely contemplative it speaks of courage and endurance of a special kind.

Here the thought of the contemplative crosses the thought of the conservationist, because the contemplative realizes that the desert is "the last frontier" in more senses than one. It is the last because it was the latest reached, but it is the last also because it is, in many ways, a frontier which *cannot* be crossed. It brings man up against his limitations, turns him in upon himself and suggests values which more indulgent regions minimize. Sometimes it inclines to contemplation men who have never contemplated before. And of all answers to the question "What is a desert good for?" "Contemplation" is perhaps the best.

The eighteenth century invented a useful distinction which we have almost lost, the distinction between the beautiful and the sublime. The first, even when it escapes being merely the pretty, is easy and reassuring. The sublime, on the other hand, is touched with something which inspires awe. It is large and powerful; it carries with it the suggestion that it might overwhelm us if it would. By these definitions there is no doubt which is the right word for the desert. In intimate details, as when its floor is covered after a spring rain with the delicate little ephemeral plants, it is pretty. But such embodiments of prettiness seem to be only tolerated with affectionate contempt by the region as a whole. As a whole the desert is, in the original sense of the word, "awful." Perhaps one feels a certain boldness in undertaking to live with it and a certain pride when one discovers that one can.

I am not suggesting that everyone should listen to the voice of the desert and listen to no other. For a nation which believes, perhaps rightly enough, that it has many more conquests yet to make, that voice preaches a doctrine too close to quietism. But I am suggesting that the voice of the desert might well be heard occasionally among the others. To go "up to the mountain" or "into the desert" has become part of the symbolical language. If it is good to make occasionally what the religious call a "retreat," there is no better place than the desert to make it. Here if anywhere the most familiar realities recede and others come into the foreground of the mind.

A world traveler once said that every man owed it to himself to see the tropics at least once in his life. Only there can he possibly realize how completely nature can fulfill certain potentialities and moods which the temperate regions only suggest. I have no doubt that he was right. Though I have never got beyond the outer fringe of the tropical lands, I hope that some day I shall get into their heart. But I am sure that they are no more necessary than the desert to an adequate imaginative grasp of the world we live in. Those who have never known it are to be pitied, like a man who has never read *Hamlet* or heard the *Jupiter Symphony*. He has missed something which is unique. And there is nothing else which can give him more than a hint of what he has missed. To have experienced it is to be prepared to see other landscapes with new eyes and to participate with a fresh understanding in the life of other natural communities.